"Living a life of purpose doesn't happen by accident. *Here I Am* will guide you toward God's plans for your life and will build your faith as you step out of your comfort zone and into His calling."

> John Lindell, lead pastor, James River Church,
> Ozark, Missouri

"In a day when the calls to 'be present' and 'all in' are heard at every turn, *Here I Am* puts the reader in play with Bible characters who show how to do just that. And Brittany Rust's candor and questions make that a profitable journey!"

> Richard Foth, coauthor (with Ruth Foth), *Known: Finding Deep Friendships in a Shallow World*

"Through the inspiring stories of the patriarchs and New Testament believers who went before us, Brittany unpacks the power of surrendering our all to God. We see through these examples that God invites us into His marvelous plan and that by our saying 'Here I am,' we, too, can experience the freedom and destiny God offers to those who want more of His presence and power in their lives—a message of hope for those who aren't satisfied with status quo."

> Kay Burnett, national women's ministries director,
> General Council of the Assemblies of God

HERE I AM

HERE I AM

Responding When God Calls Your Name

BRITTANY RUST

Chosen

a division of Baker Publishing Group
Minneapolis, Minnesota

© 2019 by Brittany Rust

Published by Chosen Books
11400 Hampshire Avenue South
Bloomington, Minnesota 55438
www.chosenbooks.com

Chosen Books is a division of
Baker Publishing Group, Grand Rapids, Michigan

Printed in the United States of America

ISBN 978-0-8007-9881-9

Library of Congress Cataloging-in-Publication Control Number: 2018053758

Cover design by Emily Weigel

Author represented by The Steve Laube Agency

19 20 21 22 23 24 25   7 6 5 4 3 2 1

To the little one we lost this season—
you are forever held in our hearts,
and without a doubt,
your life impacted this world for good.
You are so loved, always and forever.

CONTENTS

ACKNOWLEDGMENTS

Words fall short when proclaiming Your goodness and beauty. Truly, there is no one like You, God. I think about how You have impacted my life and I am in absolute awe. May my life radiate Your faithfulness and love, pointing people to You. And may this book be Yours and for Your glory. You are the Author and the only one truly able to penetrate hearts and inspire growth. I pray people would only see You, Father, in these pages and be challenged to step out in faith with their own, "Here I am, Lord." Thank You for choosing me out of Your abundant grace to be a conduit for this message.

To my handsome husband, Ryan, and son, Roman, you inspire me every day to give my all and be a Spirit-filled woman. Thank you for loving me well, cheering me on and making me better. Roman, I pray I authentically show you each day how to walk out a "Here I am" heart and that you embrace His voice above all others all the days of your life.

While writing this book, I went through the hardest season of my life. A time that included a miscarriage and a life shipwrecked on the rocks of pain and loss. I am not sure I would have made it out so well—nor would this book be as authentic—without the following people.

Mom, Dad, Austin, Zach, Kelsey and Seth, who showed up beautifully to care for our weary family.

The Assemblies of God National Women's Ministries team: Kay, Darla, Phoebe, Karlene and Hannah—who formed the most powerful prayer circle around me. Your Christlike love and care was a sweet blessing to my broken heart.

To my forever pastors, John and Debbie Lindell, and the James River Church family for being a safe haven in the storm. Your continued influence in my life regularly inspires me to carry a "Here I am" heart.

And my besties, Misty and Charity. Thank you for adopting me as your brunette sister, giving me the gift of laughter in the storm and being there for me time and again.

I love you all!

And to you, the reader. You were in my heart with every word penned and prayer prayed over this book. This book is for God and for you. I pray with all my heart you will feel challenged and inspired to step out in faith and obedience with a "Here I am" spirit. With it, I truly believe there is no end to how God will use you.

INTRODUCTION

Here I am, Lord." Little did I know when I read that phrase for the first time how much those four words would impact my life, take root deep in my soul and begin a personal spiritual awakening unlike any other.

Those four words, woven beautifully together, make up one of the most powerful phrases in Scripture. In fact, I would venture to say it is one of the most powerful phrases you or I could ever speak. But how is it that one small phrase can carry so much power? How could it radically alter your spiritual walk, igniting faith and courage, to a transformation unlike anything else? You will see!

This book will take you on a journey through your doubts, spiritual hiccups and fears to uncover what God truly wants to do in your life. It is a journey that will dive into the recesses of your soul and lead you to explore your gifts, call and purpose. God has so much He wants to do in and through you, but it takes more than just waiting for something to happen.

Living in the sweet spot of your spiritual giftings and flourishing in your God-ordained purpose involves self-discovery, honesty, pursuit of the truth, shedding the world's distractions and pursuing obedience through faith. It is more than sitting on the sidelines waiting. It is an active faith and pursuit of Him. It is walking in obedience and availability.

The Bible is full of men and women who took a step of obedience and stood firm in the face of adversity. It is full of men and women who took a stand for the cause of Christ. But there were six people in particular who exemplified what it looks like to be ready—six men who, when God called them to step out in faith, said the words, "Here I am," and responded in eager obedience. Each demonstrated what it looks like to overcome obstacles and failure to get to the point of hearing God's call and responding accordingly. Each had a bumpy road, but they show us what it looks like to overcome and try again. Each man was used to do something truly significant for the Kingdom of God as a result of uttering these three words, and history was made.

We are going to pull back the curtain on their lives and find out what made them tick. We will look at how they failed in their pursuit of righteousness, where and how God transformed their lives, and the significance of their "Here I am." My prayer is that, as a result, you will find your voice and also say, "Here I am, Lord."

However, it is not enough simply to tell the stories of these great pillars of faith and ask you to go and make your own without diving into how you can hear from God as well. The unfortunate truth is, in a world full of noises, so often people struggle to hear from God. I could inspire you with these stories and say, "Go get 'em!" but I would be doing you a disservice if I did not also help you uncover how to hear the voice of God in the first place. So, if you've always struggled to determine what is from God and what is not, to be confident if He is truly speaking to you, and to tune into His voice alone, then this book will give you valuable tools to get there. We are going to discover how to listen to God's voice and be confident when He speaks so that when He calls you, you can step out right away and flourish in your purpose. This journey begins, is sustained and ends with the voice of God beckoning you forward.

I truly believe with all my heart that God wants to show you how you can hear from Him and be a follower who is full of fierce faith and active obedience. You are holding this book in your hands for a reason, and if I were to guess why, I would say it is because God is wanting to fan into flame purpose and courage in your heart. He is ready to take you to the next level in your spiritual walk and use you like never before.

Are you ready? Are you open to this new chapter of courage and purpose God wants to write in your story? Then buckle your seat belt and let's go!

Part One

THE OBSTACLES
WE FACE

1

THE NOISES IN OUR HEADS

The sun began to rise in the east, and as light poured out onto the cool land like a blanket of warmth, the young man began to wake. He could not have been more excited. Elisha was a great prophet in the country of Israel, and he was known for many miraculous deeds. The young servant could scarcely believe that he, of all the people in the land, had been given the privilege of serving this famous man of God. It was an honor, and it was with fierce determination that he set out to serve Elisha the best he could.

Each day he awoke ready to serve his new master with excellence, and this day was no different. But as he slowly trudged forward, removing the sleepiness from his heavy eyes, he was stopped in his tracks. Looking out over the city, he saw the formidable Syrian army, a great enemy, surrounding him and Elisha. Not quite sure what was happening, he straightened himself out in alarm and took one more look for clarity before running to his master.

"Alas, my master! What shall we do?" he exclaimed, trying to keep his composure while trembling with fear on the inside. It was to his surprise that his master responded so calmly not to fear. The enemy, Elisha said, was outnumbered. But how could they be outnumbered? It was but him and his master against an army! Elisha's servant had not yet witnessed the incredible miracles he had heard so much about, and his immediate reaction in the dire situation was to fear.

Quickly the prophet Elisha began to pray, and behold, the servant instantly saw the most amazing thing his eyes had ever seen. In a split second a mountain full of horses and chariots of fire unlike anything on this earth appeared before him! With one prayer his eyes were opened to the spiritual battle that was playing out.

This account in 2 Kings 6 is a powerful reminder that there is an unseen battle in your life. If your eyes were to be opened like this servant's, you would be astonished to your very core. This man witnessed a powerful victory provided only by God and experienced a newfound peace and trust in the Father. But the battle around you is not over.

Truth is, a war is raging all around you. Powers not of flesh but of spirit are battling for your attention, resources and soul. You might not always see it happening, but it is there in the shadows, where your eyes struggle to focus, that the greatest battles are taking place. External distractions fight to capture you, keeping you locked in a constant state of tension between good and evil. Unless you remain tuned in to the voice of the Lord, you will likely find yourself paralyzed with fear, like Elisha's servant.

So, before exploring the "Here I ams" of the Bible and what it looks like to step out in faith, you must first be able to determine which voice is God's and which is not His. Noises surround you, but to step confidently into the calling God has placed on your life, you must first be able to separate God's voice from all the others. It is the only way you will hold fast to faith and peace when the battle gets close to home.

Elisha's mentor, Elijah, learned how to distinguish God's voice in a spectacular lesson, and we get a glimpse of that in 1 Kings 19:11–13, one of my favorite passages in the Bible.

> And he said, "Go out and stand on the mount before the LORD." And behold, the LORD passed by, and a great and strong wind tore the mountains and broke in pieces the rocks before the LORD, but the LORD was not in the wind. And after the wind an earthquake, but the LORD was not in the earthquake. And after the earthquake a fire, but the LORD was not in the fire. And after the fire the sound of a low whisper. And when Elijah heard it, he wrapped his face in his cloak and went out and stood at the entrance of the cave. And behold, there came a voice to him and said, "What are you doing here, Elijah?"

Elijah was faced with great acts of God—the sort of shows of power and might that many of us would presume God would use to speak. Yet, His voice came only after these demonstrations. The truth is, while the world and the enemy shout to get your attention, you will find God in the personal and intimate voice of a whisper. Elijah had learned to separate the loud external distractions from the quiet whisper of his beautiful God. Through his experience we learn so much about what we must do to move forward in our own journey. When you discover how to do the same—to identify God's voice in the chaos—you will find what you are looking for.

If you are eager to pursue what God has called you to, or even looking to figure out what that might be, first cultivate the ability to tune out all the noises but God's voice. In this chapter we will explore three external distractions fighting for your attention: the world and culture, people and the enemy. As we look at them, consider closely if any of them sound like a voice you listen to often. Gain insight into how these distractions are fighting to get between you and God, and how to combat them.

The World and Culture

This world and the culture we live in provide numerous distractions that easily entice us. These distractions have been there since the beginning of time. At first, when Adam and Eve were in the Garden, it was only them and God in perfect harmony and relationship. It was not until Satan enticed them to eat from the apple (which we will get to later) that worldly distractions first tempted humanity. At that point, when sin entered and forever changed the dynamics of our lives, the world's voice began to echo into the ears of men.

It was Adam and Eve's own sons who were first separated by this wedge. Genesis 4 tells us that Cain brought an offering of fruit to God, while his brother, Abel, brought the firstborn from their flock as an offering. God accepted Abel's sacrifice but refused his brother's. God's response was not so much about the physical offering they brought as it was the hearts behind their offering. Abel's heart was for God, but Cain's for the world. When Cain became angry at God's acceptance of Abel's offering over his, God spoke to Cain and told him that sin was crouching at the door and he had to rule over it. God was warning Cain that the world was after his heart and to fight any temptation to give in to its lure. Unfortunately, Cain did not listen to God and instead gave in to his own desires, killing his brother and separating himself from God. Cain's ego had been hurt as a result of the lies he chose to believe, and it cost him everything.

The world is summoning you to compromise, and it does so in a very sneaky way. Cloaked in promises that it knows what is best for you, it will entice you in three ways: desire, self-promotion and comparison. Let's explore how each is calling for your attention, so that you will be able to stand firm against their temptations.

Desire

Whether or not we are aware of it, desire drives so much of what we do. Though desire is not inherently sinful, when it causes you to crave something you do not have to such a degree that you strive and toil for it in order to benefit yourself, it allows sin to take root. This sinful desire results in pride, and the pursuit of validation, power, money and lust—all of which beckon us to betray God for momentary gain.

As you read about these pitfalls, remain sensitive to see if one pokes at your heart. If so, it is likely a sign that you need to develop a battle plan for overcoming this distraction and finding victory over its grip. Only when you are free from it will you be able to hear the intimate whisper of the Father.

Pride

Pride is thinking of yourself more highly than you ought to, and it often manifests in placing yourself above others. Wasn't it pride that struck at Cain's heart? His brother's offering was accepted, and his was not. *Why should that be?* he must have wondered. *Don't I deserve God's acceptance as well?* These thoughts were proud, because Cain placed himself first and foremost. In fact, even when God warned him of the sin so close to his heart, he did not repent or feel guilty; he continued down the road of revenge.

It is often said that pride is the root of all sin, and indeed it may be. Every hurt, every desire, every pursuit is prey to pride because it puts yourself first. As Rick Warren wrote, "True humility is not thinking less of yourself; it is thinking of yourself less."[1] If humility is less of yourself in the picture, then pride's voice sounds a lot like the word *me*. Pride gets you and me thinking we deserve the best and convinces us to seek after our own desires first.

Pride will call for your attention daily in the subtle and unseen moments. Giving in to it will only manifest in greater ways, and one day you will be looking at nothing but a life lived for self.

I have to admit I struggle with this more than anything perhaps. I was the oldest and only girl of a large family, and it seemed my life was devoted either to working at our family restaurant or watching one of my younger brothers. In high school I often had to give up social calls for the family. As a result, I developed a "what about me?" mentality. I worked hard, was responsible, loyal—and yet always seemed to be overlooked. This prideful attitude carried into ministry in my twenties, and it is something I have had to fight throughout adulthood.

If you find yourself struggling with a *me* mentality also, do not give up the fight. I know it is not easy, but you can gain the victory. I have found it helpful to use less *me* verbiage and more *others* verbiage. Start replacing thoughts of yourself with thoughts about God and other people. A common battle tactic: Ask yourself how you can serve another person in this situation instead of yourself. How can you put that person first? Finally, a verse I pray over myself often is Philippians 2:3–4: "Do nothing from selfish ambition or conceit, but in humility count others more significant than yourselves. Let each of you look not only to his own interests, but also to the interests of others." Renew your mind to consider others before yourself, and pride will lose a foothold in your life.

The Pursuit of Validation

Another desire is for validation, for the attention and admiration of others. Today's culture feeds into this with the instant success that can be quickly gained through social media or reality television. Someone can be famous for just about anything, and it is something many strive for. Likes and comments have become a way to measure worth.

People pursuing this desire tend to think the admiration of others will somehow fill a hole in their heart. Did someone make you feel unloved or unwanted growing up, and now you struggle to love yourself as a result? Is it that you want to be known and loved by others, so seeking the admiration of many is your pursuit? Beware: The road to fame leads nowhere of value if it is the only pursuit.

Take Instagram or YouTube, for instance. These are wonderful tools for connecting with others, but they become empty vehicles of vanity if your use for them is self-promotion. This can be an easy trap, I know. There are times I have had to step back and ask, *Is this for Jesus or for me?* If it is the latter, I know it is time to take a break. If you are heavily involved with creating an online presence or striving to gain followers, ask yourself this same honest question. If your purpose is not to lift up the name of Christ so that others would draw near, it may be time for a social media fast.

Others do not determine your worth, dear reader. Christ has that all covered. So, if you are clamoring for the recognition or admiration of others, take a step away from the tool you use to gain this. Then, once you've had your heart check and have realigned yourself, continue to ask yourself on a regular basis, Is this for Jesus, or is this for me?

Power

Power, the pursuit of authority over others, is another voice that chants proudly in our culture. The longing to be over something or someone, to have control, have the last word, be respected and to establish one's dominion is a strong enticement for many. This plays out everywhere from the world stage in politics and Fortune 500 companies to the private homes of married couples all over. Whatever the arena, the desire for power can have a devastating effect on relationships with God and people.

The thing about the pursuit of power is it often involves hurting others. It leaves hearts tattered and spirits crushed in its wake. Honestly, I do not think most people want to hurt others in their pursuit of gain; it is just that their desire to be recognized is simply misplaced.

If this is you, know there is hope for change. To get there, you must make one vital decision: release control to God. If you can learn to give control and power to Him, you will find He takes care of things much better than you can, and you will find incredible peace in this freedom. Pursue finding your importance in the Father, let go of control and feed kindness to those around you.

Money

Money is a strong enticement as well. We want the latest of everything and the best this world offers—comforts that can only be obtained through wealth. The lure of money beckons many to cut corners, railroad people and make unwise decisions for the sake of gain. Truth is, few things will show your priorities like your checkbook does.

I have a friend who once struggled with a shopping addiction for years. It locked her into a cage and drove her to hide the crippling debt from her husband for fear of his reaction. It all came out one night when she returned home from a work trip and found he had laid out her hidden credit card statements on the kitchen table.

Thankfully, my friend found both freedom from the addiction and the support she needed to overcome this pitfall. At times she still feels the urge to spend what she does not have or to seek her worth in her clothes, but then she reminds herself of her identity in Christ and the commitment she made to serve her family, not her desires.

You can find satisfaction in the eternal. And you can overcome the enticement of money. Remember not to lose sight of what really matters in this world—people—and seek to collect memories, not things. Do this, and you will find at the end of life that it will be the relationships you fostered, experiences you collected and love you cultivated that will be your most cherished assets, not your possessions.

Lust

A quick survey of ancient and modern history will highlight one truth: Lust has brought some of the mightiest to their knees. In the Old Testament alone we see a few significant examples. David saw Bathsheba and had to have her, leading to adultery, murder and the loss of a child. Solomon had hundreds of wives and concubines, who only separated him from God. Samson lost his power due to the temptations of one woman.

Today, our society treats lust like a virtue. Open almost any magazine on the stand, turn on any television show or movie, or peruse the list of bestselling novels, and you will find sex. It is everywhere you look, unfortunately, and along with it lust calls out, seeking to capture your eyes and mind.

The cost of giving in to lust is high. Sex outside of marriage takes a piece of your heart, pornography hurts a relationship and an affair can destroy a family. Do not pay this price. Momentary satisfaction is never worth the cost of a lifetime of pain and regret. Do not let this desire bring you down like a building on fire.

Desire takes many forms, and the above are only a few. If you are longing for anything outside of what God offers you, truth be told, you are hearing the whisper of the world. Tune it out—in fact, deny it—and seek the good fruit that God offers. Choose to walk in blessing and freedom, which will provide you with the ultimate joy!

Self-Promotion

The world will often tell you that you are most important. It is going to tell you to follow your heart and do what is best for you. You want that job? Do whatever it takes to get it. You want to divorce your spouse so that you can be with someone else? As long as it makes you happy. There are shows and movies dedicated to the dog-eat-dog world of advancement in the workplace, justifying self-promotion in the name of success. Self-help gurus, other religions, media—so much noise out there is directed toward convincing you to put yourself first and get ahead, whatever the cost or consequence.

This voice sounds a bit like pride and power, which we just explored. Self-promotion feeds these two. Perhaps it even serves as the introduction to pride and power, because isn't self-promotion about getting ahead anyway? It is all about you, even if it means others have to get hurt in the process.

This can be subtle. There are trains of thought that tell you to strive for holiness, but for your own sake, for your glory. Isaiah was talking about this misguidance when he said, "All our righteous deeds are like a polluted garment" (Isaiah 64:6). It is what Jesus meant when He called the Pharisees "whitewashed tombs" and told them, "You . . . outwardly appear righteous to others, but within you are full of hypocrisy and lawlessness" (Matthew 23:27–28).

Self-promotion very much contradicts what Jesus did when He came to earth. He could have come, as many believed He would, as a king on a physical throne. They believed He would come and set up shop in Israel, then proceed to have all others submit to His authority. But He did not do that, did He? Instead, He came to earth in obscurity and lived His first thirty years in relative normalcy as a carpenter. Even when He did begin His ministry, it was not with the grandeur of royalty. Jesus served others, plain and simple. He Himself said, "For even the Son of Man came not to be served but to serve, and to give his life as a ransom for many" (Mark 10:45).

When Jesus stepped into the public eye, He did so with a baptism. John the Baptist, His cousin, was preaching and baptizing hundreds when the Son of God walked up to the scene. Jesus could have asked John to step aside and used that platform—which, by the way, John would have gladly given over—as an opportunity to proclaim His authority, but He did not. Instead, standing by the very river He created, Jesus waited in line to be baptized by John. It is really incredible if you think about it.

John Eldredge paints the scene so vividly in his book *Beautiful Outlaw*:

> Picture the scene in the movie *Gladiator*—typical to the inauguration of Roman emperors—where Commodus rides into Rome on a chariot like a conquering hero. Cheering mobs line the roads—paid to attend to make a good impression. Amid all the hollow pomp, the pompous fool gives a demure wave, feigning humble acceptance of the throne. It is appalling in its arrogance.
>
> When Saddam Hussein was ousted from his dictatorship, a good deal of coverage was given to public places in Iraq. What I found particularly disgraceful were the massive idols he had erected in his honor. Murals and statues of Hussein the Magnificent were plastered all over the country—a handsome and dashing military hero, bold, a man for the people, forty years younger than he actually was. A demigod. Many dictators have done the same. Hitler did it; Chairman Mao too. It's just creepy—the self-obsession, self-exaltation, the desire to be worshipped. Yet the only king who ever had a right to be

worshipped shows up riverside at somebody else's revival and waits his turn.[2]

Jesus was not about self-promotion, though He had every right to be. In this He gives us an example to follow—an example of what it looks like to serve others instead of pass others by. Self-promotion has led many astray, and it will do that for you if you listen to its call. You have a choice to live for yourself and your own desires, or you can live for something much bigger. When you hear a *me*-centered voice within or get caught up in the allure of promotion, know this is a voice to reject and flee from. A good starting point in your escape: Do what Jesus did and serve others. Wait in line. Humble yourself for God's glory, not your own.

Comparison

Keeping up with the Joneses, or these days, the Kardashians, is a popular distraction. In fact, it has never been more popular or prevalent in our world as it is today with the media we have access to. The sad thing is, though comparison is so easy to fall into, at the same time it is one of the most destructive pitfalls. Comparison's ability to penetrate your consciousness and knock you off your path almost simultaneously is truly remarkable. Its voice calls loudest for the insecure, which I was for a long time.

I have watched comparison distract me, hurt me, discourage me and rob me of what God has put in front of me. I was made fun of quite a bit in junior high, and that only changed in high school because, to everyone's surprise, I made the dance team my freshman year. The mockery subsided, but it was still high school, and I was always comparing myself to the more popular girls. It did not end with school, either. In my early twenties

I often compared myself to the other young women in ministry. Every time another would succeed and I did not, I would inwardly wrestle with God, asking, "What about me?" I have had to fight over the years to shut out the voice of comparison and stay in the lane God has called me to.

Comparison will tell you that because someone else benefited, somehow you lost something. This is completely untrue. If you buy into this mentality, it will steer you off the course God has ordained you to follow. Christine Caine once shared a quote on Instagram that has impacted my thoughts on comparison so dramatically that I cannot help but look at it differently. She said, "Someone else's success does not rob you of anything." Instead of believing that another's win is your loss, believe that God is big enough to do abundantly more than imagined in each person's life! Make the choice to remember there is room for all of us at the table!

When you identify the voice of comparison and hear it calling your name, shut it down. Invite God into your mind, and embrace His idea of who you are—valuable. See yourself through His eyes and know that He cares deeply about you and your heart. Then, make the decision to celebrate others' wins. Overcoming comparison means rejoicing with those who rejoice. It requires patience and a sound mind, but more than anything, it requires trust in God and a heart that is committed to Him.

People

People have incredible influence in our lives. The relationships we have with others can be our biggest blessings. Think about it. What are your favorite memories of time spent with family during your growing-up years? How have your spouse and children changed your life for the better? Was there a mentor, boss or co-worker who spoke into your life and lit the path to the career or vocation God was calling you to? In a moment of deep turmoil, how did a close friend's support and counsel help bring healing to your heart and circumstances? The opinions, thoughts, advice and instruction of our friends and loved ones can change the course of our lives, even if we are not aware of it.

At the same time, relationships can also be our quickest downfall. Sometimes we give people more freedom to speak into our lives than we should. Think about some of the hard times you've had in life and what your first instinct was. For me, my immediate reaction has often been to call up my boyfriend or best friend. When trouble strikes, I often find myself craving the advice, insight or simple commiseration of those close to me. Perhaps you can relate to calling up a friend or running to a spouse the moment something got hard.

Conferring with your inner circle when you are going through tough times is not wrong, but God should always be your first point of contact, whether it is in the throes of an emergency or when you find yourself overwhelmed with gratitude. When you prioritize your relationships with others over your relationship with God, you have given people more of a foothold than you should. This imbalance will eventually have a negative effect on your life, even if the relationships and counsel you are turning to are healthy and sound.

Sometimes, however, the relationships we are drawn to are not healthy, and the counsel we receive is less than sound. There are many ways people can influence and impact your life in an unhealthy way, but there are two that are fairly common: peer pressure and people's hurt.

Peer Pressure

Peer pressure does not just happen in school and suddenly stop when you enter adulthood. Although perhaps more subtle in later years, it still creeps into your life and encourages you to compromise. This may be most evident in a romantic relationship, when compromise—and its consequences—can be more extreme, but relationships in general produce pressure whether you realize it or not.

Any time someone is prompting or encouraging or manipulating you into doing something you inwardly feel is a compromise, shut it down fast. The longer you allow that person to speak such compromise into your life, the greater the foothold you give them to lead you astray.

This sounds extreme, but it is true. I have watched godly people fall fast and hard because they allowed the wrong person to speak into their life. A co-worker talked them into going to a bar for happy hour, and they wound up passed out on the sidewalk, or worse. A boyfriend or girlfriend invited them over to an empty apartment to watch a movie, and temptation got the best of them. A fellow worship volunteer of the opposite sex suggested carpooling to an event, and an affair started. I have witnessed all three of these things happen, and these are only the beginning of a long list of possibilities.

Perhaps one of the best stories in the Bible to illustrate the dangers of peer pressure comes from 1 Samuel 15. God directed King Saul to kill every Amalekite upon defeating them so that no trace of the wicked nation would be left behind. Instead of fulfilling what God had commanded, Saul spared the best of the livestock and the king of the Amalekites. When the prophet Samuel confronted Saul about what happened, the king responded, "I was afraid of the men and so I gave in to them."

Did you catch what happened? Saul was so concerned with what his men thought of him that he became disobedient to God. It provides a powerful example of what the deep desire for men's approval can lead to. Caring about what people think, particularly above what God thinks, can lead to disobedience.

When the words or actions of another beckon you to compromise, something inside of your heart will freeze. You will know the noise of peer pressure when you hear it. You will know it when your moral compass points in the opposite direction of what they suggest. Know that this noise is contrary to God, and shut it out. Walk away from what others would have you do to compromise your calling.

People Hurt People

Sometimes it is not the advice people give but what they do that negatively impacts you. Others' actions can inflict wounds that cripple you emotionally and make it hard to hear the voice of God. Your spouse or someone you are dating might break up with you, or a friend might betray you. Someone you trust or care about deeply might take advantage of you. In the midst of such turmoil, this pain can tempt you to turn away from God and toward the world—to substance abuse, sexual immorality, anything to numb the pain—for comfort and healing. But this is not what God has for any of us.

I am speaking from personal experience. People I have unwaveringly trusted have hurt me before, and it was no easy road back to healing and forgiveness. A heart shattered and soul wounded beckoned me to bitterness. And if I am completely honest, I have not always handled those hurts well. At times, I have allowed them to knock me off course, question God, lose hope in people and find a Band-Aid in the world's cupboard for a momentary fix.

I am not the only one, either. As a result of sharing my own testimony, I have had many reach out and share their own stories of betrayal. People hurt by those they cared about and now left in ruins. People wondering how they find restoration and the ability to forgive when so deeply wounded. Being in ministry, I have watched people pull away in isolation as a result of people-inflicted wounds. They lose hope in humanity and turn to the world.

Perhaps people leave the biggest footprints in our lives. And because they affect us so, the betrayal experienced can be hard to come back from.

I want you to stop for a moment and take an inventory of your hurt. Is there any pain or scar tissue lingering as a result of not addressing the betrayal? Is there bitterness or unforgiveness attached to your heart? I would like to encourage you to do what you need to do to work through that hurt and find healing. Whether that is a verbal conversation with them, counseling or lots of prayer and worship, pursue reconciliation, at least in your heart. That kind of hurt can leave you immobile and lost if not properly dealt with. It can be a white noise that distracts and makes it hard to hear God's voice.

The Enemy

The Bible says that the enemy prowls around like a roaring lion, looking for someone to devour, and that our battle is not of this world but against powers unseen. Every day Satan and his demons are out to separate us from God. Even Jesus experienced this in the forty days after His baptism.

So the question is, How do you identify the voice of the enemy? The answer: It is any voice that says anything contrary to God! James 1:13 tells us, "Let no one say when he is tempted, 'I am being tempted by God,' for God cannot be tempted with evil, and he himself tempts no one." God does not tempt anyone. That role is reserved for the enemy.

Wasn't it Satan who tempted Adam and Eve? They had no desire to eat of the Tree of Knowledge of Good and Evil until the serpent enticed them to eat from it. He had them questioning what God had said, even though they clearly knew God's word on the matter. Satan made it enticing to sin, and it worked. Adam and Eve both took a bite, and sin entered the world.

Satan wants to get into your head and plant thoughts and suggestions that will propel you down a dangerous path or deter you from God. Sometimes—in fact, often—the enemy's voice sounds a lot like your own. The judgment of another person passes through your mind. A beautiful woman or handsome man flirts with you, and you play into the conversation. You think about picking up a bottle of alcohol when things get tough, in spite of years of sobriety. If there is anything inside of you—a thought, inclination, feeling—that is contrary to God's Word, then it must be of the enemy.

Sometimes it may be more subtle. The enemy may whisper, "Sleep in and stay home from church today. You've worked hard." But then after you give in, it turns into a weekly habit. Or perhaps he convinces you to buy into the lie that being a good person is the path to heaven. "God loves everybody," he might say. "Why would He allow a good person to go to hell just because they did not believe in Him?" There are so many ways the enemy tempts us—too numerous to list—which is why you must pay attention to your heart when your moral compass begins pointing in another direction.

Identifying the enemy as the source of these thoughts is the first significant step. The next is dealing with them.

How to Combat These Noises

Now that you can identify external distractions and those voices that run contrary to God's Word, what do you do? How do you drown them out so that it is God's voice alone you follow? The answer is really rather simple: Tune in to God's voice! There are three things you can start doing today to cultivate this ability to listen to Him alone.

Read the Bible

There is no better way to identify the voice of God than to be in His Word. Reading the Bible is absolutely, hands down, the best way to learn what He is about, what He desires and how He approaches life! If you want to learn how to distinguish His voice among all the other voices, you must be in the Word as much as possible.

Did you know that people who read the Bible three times a week or less are no less likely to engage in sin than those who do not read the Bible at all? Research has shown that the magic number is four. If you can read the Bible at least four times a week, you are roughly 50–75 percent less likely to engage in sin.[3] It is why being in the Word is so important. It is a tool to defeat the enemy in moments of temptation. It discerns what is right and wrong. It guides us into a flourishing life. And it brings us closer to Jesus. The Bible is God's only definitive word. Second Timothy 3:16–17 (NLT) says,

> All Scripture is inspired by God and is useful to teach us what is true and to make us realize what is wrong in our lives. It corrects us when we are wrong and teaches us to do what is right. God uses it to prepare and equip his people to do every good work.

Take time every day to read. Some days will be harder or busier than others, but at least get something in you. Download a Bible app on your phone and read the verse of the day when you wake up each morning. Take a chapter a day and dive into the lesson it has for you. I like to read a portion each day and find one thought I can meditate on until the next morning. You will learn so much about our mighty God, be impacted more than you imagine and grow a great deal through this practice.

The Bible is God's definitive Word, and when you read it, you can know with certainty you are hearing from Him. Get His Word in you, and His voice will become much clearer.

Pray

Prayer is a conversation between you and God, plain and simple. It is not lofty words or deep, theological breakdowns; it is the unfiltered and vulnerable thoughts you share with Him.

When you spend time with God, coupled with studying Scripture, you learn a great deal about identifying His voice. How so? As you know, conversation is necessary for any relationship. It is how you learn about another, share your heart and cultivate intimacy. Through intimacy you recognize the voice and heart of another. I know my husband's voice when he is across a room full of people. I can instantly know which of my three brothers is on the phone just by hearing their simple "hello." It is because I have spent time with them and know them that I can identify their voices. Likewise, in prayer, you develop intimacy with God through communication.

When I was a teenager new to the faith, my youth pastor, Scotty Gibbons, would often say, "The battle is won in prayer." At the time, prayer was a foreign concept to me. It was amazing to me that I could talk to God, but I was not quite sure what that looked like. Was I supposed to be on bowed knees or pacing the floor? Was it silently, in my head, or loudly, with enthusiasm? Was it with my hands folded gently before me or with arms lifted high in surrender? It was not just these "hows" of prayer either; it was the when, where and frequency that left me confused.

Perhaps I should identify what prayer is not. Prayer is not simply

- a Get Out of Jail Free card,
- the last option when all else fails,
- something you do only when you need a request from God,
- a place to be disrespectful,

- or something to quickly pass over with a few rushed words.

E. M. Bounds wrote in *Purpose in Prayer*, "We can never get to know Him if we use the vehicle of prayer as we use the telephone—for a few words of hurried conversation. Intimacy requires development."[4]

Prayer should not play second fiddle in your day, but instead be cherished as a priority. It is prayer that touches the throne of God. It is prayer that turns your situation upside down. It is prayer that changes things. I am able to stand by this because I have watched it play out time and again in my own life.

The Bible says in 1 Thessalonians 5:17 to "pray without ceasing." Some may look at that and immediately be discouraged, because how is one supposed to pray without ceasing? I breathed a sigh of relief when I learned it did not mean to pray without stopping, but rather to cultivate a lifestyle of prayer. It means our days should be filled with instances of prayer, whether that is a devoted time in the morning, while you are sitting in your car, when a dilemma pops up or when you are about to have a meal. Prayer should be the natural outflow of a life surrendered to Christ.

So prompt yourself to pray, at every turn and silent moment, so that you form an intimate bond with your Creator.

Practice

The third thing you can do to cultivate an ear for God's voice is to practice it. One thing we are going to find in our exploration of the "Here I am" phrases is that the people who said it failed quite a bit leading up to that definitive moment. They failed because they struggled to identify God's voice among all the other noises. They listened to the wrong voice and, in that failure, learned what was not God's voice. However, they stepped out in other situations and ultimately discovered what God's voice was indeed.

You may shudder at thinking failure can be good. After all, we often fear failure, don't we? I am not saying that failure is preferable; however, there is no failure too big for God to redeem. It is a wonderful conduit for learning and growth if you will allow it to be. Failure will show you where to pivot and make a change. It does not mean you will sit at rock bottom forever. God sees you when you misstep, and He promises to be with you and to set your feet on solid ground when you are shaken. He will not abandon you, and if you will allow Him to speak into your life, He will use even your failures for good.

Practice honing your ability to hear His voice. When you feel a prompting in your spirit you think might be God, go for it! The more you step out in faith, the more you will feel comfortable with His voice. I have experienced this when I have felt prompted to go talk to a stranger or step out in a new endeavor, and although I heard many other contradictory voices, like fear and doubt, I stepped out to discover it was God all along!

When, like Elisha's servant, all you can see and hear are the sounds of the enemy's armies marching toward you, do not be afraid. Do not allow yourself to become disoriented or lose heart as a result of the noise from the adversary of your soul. Turn your ear to God. Listen for His voice. Listen for His peace. Lock on to His loving whispers. And then step out in faith and obedience, walking in the calling He has for your life.

2

FEAR AND DOUBTS
AND INSECURITY, OH MY!

Have you ever noticed it is often your strongholds you find comfort in and hold dear? They are the carry-on baggage you keep close on the journey because they are worn in and familiar. At times they seem to have almost merged with your DNA, making you believe they are part of your identity. Yet, nothing could be further from the truth.

For me, it was a stronghold of anger that held me in chains. I adopted it at a young age while living in a tense home, and it was my coping mechanism, protector and outlet for all the negativity in my life. It was my buffer against the world, and I came to believe that I needed it close in order to survive. It was not until I became a believer in my teenage years that I realized just how harmful it was. In spite of this revelation, it took me a few years after giving my heart to Jesus to find a sort of freedom. I had held it close for many years, and releasing it was a hard lesson. One I am still learning to master in certain seasons.

But it was one I had to learn. Romans 6:12 shares, "Let not sin therefore reign in your mortal body, to make you obey its passions." I knew that I could never experience the full life God had planned for me as long as anger held me captive, stuck in a cycle of disobedience.

In the first chapter we dove into external distractions that prevent you from stepping into the plans God has for you. In this chapter we are going to look at how fear, doubt and insecurity beckon you to live in a world of limitations instead of in the freedom to pursue your calling. Though they are familiar, these internal distractions are quite dangerous and can be instruments for sin. It is time to become aware of them so they do not control you and so that you can master them.

Fear

Fear is a common distraction. Whatever your struggle, there is a connection to a deep-seated fear. In fact, because fear is so deeply engrained into the flesh, it is the root of all sin in your life.

For example, a fear of not being good enough can manifest into the need for recognition, thus igniting pride in your heart. The fear of losing control can lead to bursts of anger when things do not go as planned. A fear of rejection from a loved one can drive you to find acceptance from another person or lead you to lustful thoughts that entice you to view pornography. The fear of not being accepted may tempt you to gossip so that others might be perceived in a negative light instead of you. Rest assured, whatever the sin, fear is at the root.

If you can recognize the areas of fear that are leading to sin in your life, then you can destroy it at the root. The first step is to identify the fears in your life that hinder you from stepping out into obedience when God calls your name. If you can identify one or two that you struggle with particularly, then you will be better informed and equipped to fight the fear. Here are four common types of fear that become obstacles to obedience.

Fear of Failure

A guy resists asking a girl out on a date because he might be rejected. An employee fears asking for a much-deserved raise because he might be denied. A young person never even applies to the school she is interested in because she is afraid she would not get in anyway. And what about you? How often do you fear the possibility of failure? Do you hesitate to step forward simply because you have no assurance of success?

The fear of failure plays out when you resist pursuing a dream God has put on your heart because what if it does not work out? No one wants to fail, so this lie often does the trick in limiting the potential of a believer's life.

I think the reason we truly fear failure is because we perceive success or failure as a barometer of our value or worth. So, because we do not want any external indication to reinforce an internal fear that we might not measure up, we simply do not try. We stay where we are because it is safe and more comfortable than taking a risk only to find out we do not measure up to the task, or worse, simply are not good enough.

Does any of this sound familiar or hit a sensitive spot within you? If so, it is important for you to know that your contribution to the Kingdom of God can never grow if you stay exactly where you are. In Matthew 25, Jesus shares the Parable of the Talents. In the story, three men are given talents by their master before the master goes on a journey. While the master is gone, two of the men invest their talents, while one buries his. Then the master returns and asks for an account of the talents—what did the men do with what was entrusted to them? The two men who invested their talents were rewarded as faithful servants.

The one who did not invest was admonished for not investing what was given to him. The master declared these harsh words in verse 27: "Then you ought to have invested my money with the bankers, and at my coming I should have received what was my own with interest."

Jesus is looking for people who will invest what is entrusted to them. When He returns and asks for an account, He will be interested to hear if you invested your talents. Think of it this way: By your playing it safe, how many people will never experience the contribution you could add to their lives? How many people will miss out on a life-changing encounter with the living God because you were too scared to show them what it looks like to live in total surrender and freedom?

Do not fear failure and what could happen if you tried. Maybe you will fail, but rest assured, that is not an indication of your worth. What does matter is what you do with what you have. Jesus is looking for you to step out and invest into the Kingdom. Will you?

Fear of Leaving the Comfortable

Comfort is a beautiful thing. It is a word you just want to snuggle up to, am I right? We all love our comfort food, comfy blankets and cozy homes. Comfort is a major driver, and for good reason. It screams good things.

As wonderful as comfort can be, it can also be dangerous. Comfort can feel so good that it ends up hurting so bad. "How?" you might ask. Because like the fear of failure, comfort keeps you exactly where you are and prevents you from going any-where else.

There is a word for staying in one place: *stagnation*. It is the same word used to describe a murky pond that goes nowhere. Did you know that stagnation is a breeding ground for disease? True story. And not just physically, but spiritually. Stay in one place because of fear, and your soul will ache. Your destiny will spoil. Purpose will be lost in the stagnation.

If you really want to do something in the Kingdom of God, you must be willing to step out of your comfort zone. You have to adopt a mentality that you will still go when your flesh pleads to stay. The only way to go where you never imagined you would be able to is to get up and fight for it.

Fear of the Unknown

I know all about the emotions that can overwhelm you when the unfamiliar comes knocking on your door. Not knowing what is next or what is out there can cause debilitating fear. You are not the only one, friend.

Thrillers and sci-fi movies use this to their advantage all the time. Whenever I watch them—which, honestly, is almost never because I am a big ol' scaredy-cat—they get me yelling at the characters on the TV to stay where they are instead of investigating the source of some strange noise. Who knows what is out there? In real life, while the situations are different from these movies, the fear is the same.

Not knowing what is ahead can indeed be scary, but that does not mean what is ahead is not good. You will only truly experience the phrase "the best is yet to come" when you become open to what is next. Are you willing to miss the abundance God has simply because you do not know what might happen on the journey? Know that all things have purpose in God's Kingdom—the good and the bad. With God on your side, you are a conqueror no matter what comes.

Do not forget the journey of faith is just that—a journey by faith. You cannot walk this life by sight only. You must walk by faith, which means when you cannot see what is ahead, take the hand of Jesus and trust Him to lead you. Have a faith that steps out and follows God, sight unseen.

Fear of Others

The fear of what others think or how they will respond is another tool the enemy uses to keep us bound and prevent us from stepping into the great call of God on our lives. When this fear creeps into your mind, replace it with this statement of fact: No one but God determines my worth, and no one can hinder what God wants to do in me and through me. If God is for me, then who can be against me?

There are numerous stories in the Bible that tell a tale of fear. Many of those deal with the fear of others. As we learned earlier, Saul feared his men, so he was disobedient in his call to thoroughly defeat the enemy. Peter was afraid of the mob and soldiers after the arrest of Jesus, and in that place of fear, he denied Christ three times. Both Abraham and Isaac told people their wife was a sister out of fear that men might kill them to have their wives.

The enemy will tell you to fear man, but in reality, if God has called you to go, then He will take care of you. When Jonah went to Nineveh, he stepped into a culture that was deeply sinful. Many people did, in fact, fear people from this city. But God had called Jonah to the wicked nation and protected him every step of the way.

Knowing this fear of others exists, God wrote in Proverbs 29:25, "The fear of man lays a snare, but whoever trusts in the LORD is safe." The truth is, people are often much scarier in our minds than they really are. Do not allow this fear to keep you from loving them.

Freedom from Fear

While writing this book I went through one of the hardest seasons of my life—perhaps the hardest. I was already in a place of confusion and pain when suddenly I found myself facing a major decision, one that would have major implications for the trajectory of my life. I have never faced such extensive spiritual warfare before, and it was overwhelming at times. Thankfully, God saw me through and used the experience to teach me something incredibly valuable about fear—something you might need to hear.

In the process of trying to discern God's will for me in that situation, I became paralyzed with a fear that I would make the wrong decision and forever impact my family and calling in a negative way. This fear soon gave birth to another: Why was I not hearing clearly from God? Locked in this debilitating state of mind, I found myself doubting myself and my connection with Him.

Then I read a book that released me to move forward. It's called *How to Survive a Shipwreck* by Jonathan Martin, and its words are soothing and clarifying for anyone going through a storm or who finds their life shipwrecked. It helped me navigate my own tempest, and I am not quite sure what I would have done without it. God used the following passage to bring me freedom:

> God is not on the other side of any particular door passively waiting; he is on the other side of all the doors, eager to be discovered, and better yet, he is on this side of the door with you right here, right now—for you and not against you.[1]

Until I read this, I believed that of the two options before me, only one would lead me into God's purposes. I had bought into the notion that He would only be on the other side of one decision and lived in fear I would go the wrong direction and completely thwart God's plan for my life. But the truth is, I am not big enough to thwart His plan. I am not powerful enough to throw His good plan into chaos. None of us is. When I embraced the truth that God is with me now and will be with me on the other side of any decision because He loves me, fear lost its grip on me.

It is a fact of life that sometimes you may not always hear His voice so clearly. You might seek it and struggle to find it, like I did. It does not mean God is not there, but sometimes He simply goes quiet for a reason. His silence is purposeful.

God gave each and every one of us the ability to make our own decisions. But this free will is not an endorsement to live however we want. He wants us to seek His will. But if our hearts are truly His and we seek after Him, then His desires become our desires. His will becomes our natural pleasure. Then when forks appear in the road before us and we pray with all our heart with no answer, the decision is ours to make. If we are truly after His heart and will, and He seems quiet, then we must trust that He will honor the decision we make. Martin explains it this way:

> You're not a pawn on a chessboard, mindlessly being moved by a higher power. You are called to be "God's fellow workers." You get a say in the kind of life you want to live, the kind of person you want to become, the kind of work you want to do.[2]

When God calls us "fellow workers" in 1 Corinthians 3:9, it means He wants you and me to step fully into our role as co-laborers and stop sitting on the sidelines. This freedom to make our own choices, guided by His will, is a gift, and I cannot help but wonder if He goes quiet sometimes to see how we will respond.

Fellow brother or sister in Christ, do not allow fear to paralyze you. Do not become immobile because you believe there is only one way to pursue the calling on your life. Know that God's silence is not an indication of His proximity to you; it could be a beautiful call to step into Kingdom work as a co-laborer. Your partnership with the Father is a mutual, loving relationship. It's not a do-this-or-else kind of life He extends but rather a call to work with Him to bring good news to the poor, bind up the brokenhearted and proclaim liberty to the captives. I don't know about you, but I am excited that this is the kind of relationship God invites us into—a relationship of intimacy, adventure, purpose and mutual labor.

Step forward and follow God where you believe He is leading. Maybe you will go, and it does not quite work out like you had hoped. That is okay. You are in good company. Every one of the men and women we read about in this book were ordinary people who made mistakes, just like you and me. They made bad calls and went in questionable directions, but God still used them. He was still with them on the other side of the door and used all things for good. I am confident He will do the same for you and me.

You were not made to fear anyone or anything. If any of the fears we have talked about is an entanglement for you, then only you, by the power of the Holy Spirit, can overcome it. Second Timothy 1:7 declares, "For God gave us a spirit not of fear but of power and love and self-control." You have been given power and love and self-control—fear not included!

Take heart in the words spoken by God in Isaiah 41:10: "Fear not, for I am with you; be not dismayed, for I am your God; I will strengthen you, I will help you, I will uphold you with my righteous right hand." God is with you and has you, no matter what might be ahead. Fear not.

Doubts

For some reason, we think of doubt and worry as "small" sins. But when a Christian displays unbelief . . . or an inability to cope with life, he is saying to the world, "My God cannot be trusted," and that kind of disrespect makes one guilty of a fundamental error, the heinous sin of dishonoring God. That is no small sin.[3]

John MacArthur

Doubt is a troubling thing. As MacArthur stated, we may think of doubt as a small sin, but in reality, it is a sign of unbelief in our God. How dangerous this can be in your life if it is allowed control, no matter how little.

Doubt manifests itself in two ways: when you doubt yourself and when you doubt God.

Doubting Yourself

I have doubted myself many times, more than I can count (or care to remember). It comes from a mind-set that says, "I'm not good enough to accomplish the task" or "I'm incapable of doing it as well as another," and stems from a doubt in your ability to perform. Unless it is dealt with, self-doubt will limit your contributions to this world.

Have you struggled with this like I have? Perhaps for you it was less obvious. Sometimes self-doubt manifests as false humility. We tell ourselves, "She is really so much better at that than I am. I'll just let the pros handle it." In reality, we are hyperfocused on our own shortcomings to the degree that we put ourselves and our doubts before what God is calling us to do.

When God asks you to step out in faith and obedience, what is your first thought? Do you reply with, "Here I am, Lord"? Or do you find yourself making excuses? Perhaps you tell Him:

"I'm not as good at that as she is."
"I could never do that well."
"I'm not equipped for such a task."

These statements express doubt in your ability to do anything well for the Kingdom of God. In reality, it is doubting that God can use you regardless of your experience. The enemy would like it very much if you chose to live with this mind-set, but Jesus certainly does not want you limited by your own beliefs about your ability to perform. This is when it comes in handy to have Philippians 4:13 memorized: "I can do all things through him who strengthens me." Even if you may be weak, Jesus has all the strength you will never need.

It is important to remember that God can and will use you no matter what you might believe about your worth (or lack of it). It is time to free yourself up from this limiting mind-set and shake off any doubt you might have in your ability.

Doubting God

Let's get brutally honest with each other. Have you ever believed for God to move on your behalf in a particular way, and He did not? If God did not show up for you like you wanted when you asked Him to, it is possible you are going through life doubting on some level that He will come through for you. While you still believe in Him and His goodness, you have given up on Him. So, instead of stepping out in faith, you only move by sight, and you make plans and take action without giving serious consideration to what God wants for you and how He might want to use you. As with self-doubt, the lack of trust in God that is at the root of this doubt is inherently dishonoring to God.

I have to ask you, Is that what you really want? Is that how you prefer to go through life, not trusting Him? Or is it your desire to shake off this doubt and start trusting Him again, to knock down the wall you have built around your heart and embrace a vulnerability with Him you have long forgotten? Do you crave sweet intimacy and trust with Him again? If so, there is hope.

You can choose not to limit God through your unbelief. Will you choose today to believe that God can do far more in and through you than you could ever imagine? Yes? Then make Ephesians 3:20 (MESSAGE) your mantra:

> God can do anything, you know—far more than you could ever imagine or guess or request in your wildest dreams! He does it not by pushing us around but by working within us, his Spirit deeply and gently within us.

Allow Him to work deeply and gently within you, removing the hardened wall built up around your heart and using you in a way that is not limited by a doubt in who He is.

Dumping Doubt

Job had a lot of time to think after he lost everything. Near the end of his ordeal, he realized he got a few things wrong in his examination of how he handled his great loss.

> I know that you can do anything, and no one can stop you. You asked, "Who is this that questions my wisdom with such ignorance?" It is I—and I was talking about things I knew nothing about, things far too wonderful for me. You said, "Listen and I will speak! I have some questions for you, and you must answer them." I had only heard about you before, but now I have seen you with my own eyes. I take back everything I said, and I sit in dust and ashes to show my repentance.
>
> Job 42:1–6 NLT

This is Job's declaration of confession and repentance. In this raw moment, he finally realized he had been questioning God's sovereignty and wisdom. He now saw that he had doubted his mighty God by questioning why he was going through such terrible things.

The key to overcoming doubt, as we see in this passage, is a humble heart. Job did not have all the answers as to why he was suffering, but he did finally have perspective on the greatness and glory of God. So, Job repented and sought restoration through humility, even though his circumstances had not changed.

I have come to understand this all too well since suffering a miscarriage recently. Before I found out I was pregnant, life did not seem like it could get much worse. My husband and I were in the middle of a very difficult season, so when we found out we were expecting our second child, it was a ray of sunshine. That little life growing inside me was a beautiful blessing. But after nine weeks in the womb, our little one's heart stopped beating. That loss was one of the most traumatic experiences I have endured. Life did, indeed, get worse.

The two weeks between when we found out the baby's heart had stopped and when I lost the pregnancy brought a lot of doubt about the character of God. I questioned how any good could come from this loss, and as a result I wondered if He was really good. I questioned if this was a punishment of sorts and if God really loved me. Much like Job, in the little understanding I had, I called into question the sovereignty of God. But then I pressed in and found my sweet Jesus. I do not have all the answers, and no, I do not know what is best. But He does. I learned firsthand that God can be trusted with every aspect of my life and will always bring some good out of the most difficult situations life has to offer. But it took humbling myself and dumping the doubt to experience His peace.

If you are prone to doubting yourself or God in difficult times or moments of stepping out, choose a different path. Shut out the voice of doubt and embrace humility. Embrace that God wants to do something in and through you, and He is calling you for "such a time as this." Will you sit paralyzed in your unbelief? Or will you embrace a posture that reflects a belief that God is great, He is good and He is calling you to step out for His purposes?

Insecurity

Insecurity may be one of the most common internal distractions we face. While self-doubt leads you to question your performance, insecurity leads you to question your value. One is an external manifestation, and one is an internal perception.

Insecurity certainly was an ugly, unwelcomed companion in my life for many years. In fact, there is one particular phrase that still echoes in my mind like a broken record under certain circumstances. It is the phrase, "I am not good enough." To this day, it is the internal distraction I fight most, the one thing I have the hardest time shaking. Maybe a similar phrase plays frequently in your mind, and it is so familiar that it feels like an old comrade keeping you company.

Believing you are not good enough has a particularly devastating effect on your life. Imagine you give yourself one hundred percent to a passion, only to get overlooked. You want to give up because it seems there is no point. Or perhaps you try to do something romantic for your spouse, but it falls flat. You internalize it, assuming it means you are not loving well. Before long, you are no longer living out your full potential.

When you put stock in your insecurities and give them validity, you are allowing pieces of your potential to be chipped away. The truth is, God never wants you to feel inadequate or not good enough. He wants you to be aware of your weakness so that you might lean into His strength, but never for a second does He want you to diminish your own value.

I get goosebumps when I read The Message translation of 1 Peter 2:9–10. It says that we are chosen by God, not for ourselves but to be an example of His power to take you "from nothing to something, from rejected to accepted." You are something. You are accepted. Do not allow insecurity to diminish your potential or steal away your calling. They will if you do not keep careful guard over your heart and mind. Remember, if

God is calling you to do something for Him, you can do it! God equips those He calls.

Finding the Freedom to Step Out

You may still be wondering, How do I know with confidence that it is God asking me to step out? I will break it down as clearly as I can for you, but first you must know there will likely always be a little mystery when you step out. That is the very definition of a life lived by faith. You have to be willing to step in the direction you feel God is calling you—and trust that if you get it wrong, He will still be with you, help you learn from the experience and pick you back up.

Stepping out begins with honing in on His voice. This goes back to the end of the last chapter: Read the Bible, pray and practice. Doing these three things will help you tune out the external voices so that you can better hear His. These are the three most important habits to embrace when learning to live by faith.

Next, separate your emotions from His voice. Ask yourself, Are my feelings clouding my judgment? If there is the smallest yes, stop and wait. Put the brakes on. Do not follow your heart; follow His voice.

This means you will have to find freedom from your emotions. It is time to stop allowing them to direct your path. It is time to stop following your heart, because the Word says it is deceitful above all else. The world does not realize that following your heart only leads to heartache.

To be clear, I am not saying, "Down with emotions entirely!" because they can be good. They were given to you by the Creator for a reason. But as Jon Bloom aptly points out, "God designed your emotions to be gauges, not guides."[4] Emotions are there because they have a way of bringing joy and protecting you from harm, but emotions and internal distractions should never stop you from stepping out.

Finally, choose carefully whom you allow to speak into your life. There will be people who tell you not to go when God is calling you to step out and vice versa, but His voice should come first. Weigh carefully the input of others. If you are married, trust your spouse as you discern God's direction for your family. Let me say from experience: If it is a major decision, and both spouses are not fully in, do not go forward. Two have become one—trust your spouse.

Above all, remember that when you trust God and step out in obedience to Him, He will cause you to flourish beautifully.

> But blessed are those who trust in the LORD and have made the LORD their hope and confidence. They are like trees planted along a riverbank, with roots that reach deep into the water. Such trees are not bothered by the heat or worried by long months of drought. Their leaves stay green, and they never stop producing fruit.
>
> Jeremiah 17:7–8 NLT

Be like the tree planted by the water. You will remain firmly planted and will not worry when heat or drought comes calling. No matter what, you know where your hope is found and will remain confident so that no distraction can lead you away from the flowing waters and promised care provided by the Father.

We opened this chapter with Romans 6:12. It seems fitting we should end with the verses that follow:

> Let not sin therefore reign in your mortal body, to make you obey its passions. Do not present your members to sin as instruments for unrighteousness, but present yourselves to God as those who have been brought from death to life, and your members to God as instruments for righteousness. For sin will

have no dominion over you, since you are not under law but under grace.

Romans 6:12–14

Grace redeemed you, brought you from death to life. You no longer belong to yourself or sin but instead belong to Him and are now an instrument for righteousness. Oh, reader, please do not allow sin to have dominion over you in any way. No emotion or internal distraction can be allowed to rule in your heart. It is time to stop giving room for these hindrances to have a voice, and start following the voice of God.

Learning to discern His voice over all the external and internal voices looking to distract you from your purpose is one of the most important things you can do. You must master this discipline in order to fully step into the call on your life. Be like Elijah and learn to hear His gentle whisper over the distractions clamoring for attention around you. There is where you will find Him.

Part Two

PEOPLE WHO RESPONDED IN OBEDIENCE

3

ABRAHAM, THE PATRIARCH

The "Here I Am" of Sacrifice

ave you ever had to give up someone or something you really cared about? Or perhaps that dear thing was taken from you. For most of us traveling this journey called life, this deeply felt challenge has happened a time or two. I have had it happen to me more than once, unfortunately. It was painful, even brutal. The pain, despair and sometimes hopelessness of it all were overwhelming to the point I almost gave up. It was not easy by any means, and I bet many of you can relate to that kind of tearing of the soul when life is so hard that few things soften the blow. It was in those moments of silence and anguish, however, that God was most real to me. If you can relate to the pain of that kind of loss, you can probably relate to the intimacy with God that accompanies such a time.

There is a man in the Bible who knew all too well the cost of sacrifice, as well as the reward for clinging closely to God. His name is Abraham.

Before exploring Abraham's profound "Here I am" moment, let's go back to the beginning of his story. We all have a background that explains so much of who we are, don't we? Abram first appears in Genesis 11, where we read that he was living with his father, Terah. Joshua 24:2 tells us that Terah "served other gods" and was living in the land of debauchery known as Babylon. This means Abram, the great patriarch of Israel, came from a godless home in a wicked nation.

This humble beginning is relatable, but it also contains an encouraging lesson: It does not matter who you were or where you come from. It does not matter if the beginning of your story involves poverty, abuse, violence or loss. It does not even matter if God was absent from your past. What matters is that when God chooses a person, regardless of situation, anything is possible. And so it was for Abram, a man who started out with little and became one of the greatest men ever to live—a nobody who became an example for all.

Acts 7:2–4 recounts that at some point while Abram and Terah were in Ur (in Babylon), God spoke to Abram and told him to "go into the land that I will show you" (v. 3). This is the beginning of his faith journey; the moment he made a choice to be different. Abram decided to believe God and follow Him instead of the false gods worshiped in Ur. It was not necessarily the easiest introduction either, since God had commanded Abram to convince his family to leave and travel to another land. Though Abram could not have known the significance of it then, this new land was Canaan, the Promised Land.

While Abram did leave Ur, he was not completely obedient and did not make the full journey. For some reason we are not made aware of, Abram stopped just shy of the boundary to the Promised Land and settled in Haran, a trading town along the Euphrates River in Mesopotamia.

Once again, Abram's story is relatable. Too often we get a sense that God is calling us somewhere and we begin that unknown journey, only to settle when we find a comfortable spot along the way instead of reaching the final destination. I can tell you I have been there, done that. As easy as it is, it is not okay to settle once we find a place we like. When God calls you to do something or to go somewhere specific, stopping halfway for comfort or giving up because of exhaustion is not an option in God's eyes. Maybe you are thinking there is little harm in pausing or taking a break. Unfortunately, delayed obedience is still disobedience. Thankfully, God does not give up on us when we disobey. God did not give up on Abram either and called his name again to give him another chance to walk in obedience.

In Genesis 12:1–4 we get a glimpse into the first recorded conversation between God and Abram. We find him in Haran with his wife, Sarai, with Lot and his family, as well as an abundance of servants and flocks. He was living very well, with lots of possessions and riches, when God's mighty voice interrupted his comfortable life.

> Now the LORD said to Abram, "Go from your country and your kindred and your father's house to the land that I will show you. And I will make of you a great nation, and I will bless you and make your name great, so that you will be a blessing. I will bless those who bless you, and him who dishonors you I will curse, and in you all the families of the earth shall be blessed."
> So Abram went, as the LORD had told him, and Lot went with him. Abram was seventy-five years old when he departed from Haran.

In these three sentences, God called Abram to go. Specifically, God told Abram to "go from . . . your father's house." Essentially, He was telling Abram to sever the comfort he had clung to. For Abram, abandoning what was comfortable in order to obey God's call was key to stepping into the promises of God. That act of obedience was the first step in a long and fruitful journey with God.

Interestingly enough, in those three sentences in Genesis 12, God used the phrase "I will" five times. Five times in three sentences is a signal for us to pay attention. It means God has something very important to communicate. Are you listening? Good. As God was calling Abram to leave what was comfortable and embark on a journey into the unknown, He was reassuring Abram that He would take care of him. "I will" was a promise of faithfulness. God was asking Abram to step out in faith while also making it very clear that He would do the work. He was bringing Abram from worldly comfort to true security in Him. This interaction and the promise it contains formed the foundation for God's calling of Abraham to sacrifice Isaac.

In case you forgot to insert yourself into this story, take a moment now to do so. Do you know that God has a plan for you? It is true! He has a plan to give you a hope and a future. The actuality of that plan does require some things from you though. Most notably, God is going to require that you separate yourself from the comforts in this world.

In my own life there have been times when I became too comfortable with someone or something, and in those instances, God took me through situations that caused me to sever unhealthy connections so that I could recalibrate and set my focus on Him. One instance that comes to mind happened when I was 23 years old. I was working for a very large church that I would have happily stayed at forever. However, God had a different plan, and through a series of events, He made it very clear He had something else for me besides my own settled plan. I was not sure what that was exactly, but I knew I needed to be obedient. On a whim I applied for a job at a resort ranch in the mountains of Wyoming. I ended up getting the job, and within two weeks I packed up all the clothes and books I had into my little Volkswagen and began a three-day journey out west.

For a girl who had rarely traveled, let alone driven so far alone, this was a huge step of faith for me. I could not see what would happen, and most people in my life were telling me not to go. But I could not ignore that quiet voice telling me I had to. With all the other voices clamoring for attention in my life, it barely got me out the door, but it was just enough. That summer in Wyoming ended up being one of the best things I ever did, and God used it in ways that would take a whole book to describe.

Just as it was hard for Abram to leave the comfort of Haran, it was hard for me to leave home and travel halfway across the country to a place I had never been. But I learned, like Abram, that when God tells you to go, He will certainly be with you. I saw that played out so vividly that summer, as God used me to love and serve over a hundred young adults from all over the world who did not know Jesus.

I also learned from that experience that if God is prompting you to sever yourself from what is comfortable, do it right away. Trust me; it is far easier to do it now instead of hesitating. Chances are, hesitating will bring about a difficult situation that will force it and, in the end, make it harder for you. Take it from a stubborn gal like me; it is much better to listen and go than to be forced. A far better place and a more intimate relationship with God are waiting on the other side of your decision to trust and obey Him now.

Trying to Do What Only God Can Do

Let's return to the story of Abram and fast-forward ten years. In the decade since leaving Haran, Abram entered Canaan, traveled to Egypt due to a famine, traveled back to Canaan, split from Lot, rescued Lot and received the famous promise that he would be given a son and heirs as numerous as the stars in the sky. It was quite the journey for our patriarch, to say the least.

This brings us to Genesis 16, smack dab in the middle of a family mess. Coming off the heels of God's covenant promise, we see Abram and Sarai take matters into their own hands. For years the couple had tried and prayed for their own child, someone they could bring into the world, love tremendously and raise as their own. God had promised Abram a son, and neither Abram nor Sarai were about to give up on that dream. Hope was wearing thin, and time was running out.

In an attempt to get the ball rolling—perhaps just give a nudge to God's plan—Sarai hatched a scheme. The story unfolds a bit dramatically. She went to her beloved husband and suggested he marry her Egyptian servant, Hagar, in order to conceive a son. You can probably smell trouble already. Astonishingly, Abram agreed, and not too surprisingly, Hagar became pregnant with a son.

Instead of bringing their family peace and joy, the enemy used that innocent baby to drive a wedge between them. Hagar developed contempt in her heart toward Sarai, so Sarai began to treat Hagar poorly, which made Hagar decide to run away toward Egypt. I know; it is like a soap opera.

While en route, Hagar eventually ended up near a spring in the wilderness and had an encounter with God. In their conversation, two things happened: God told Hagar to name the son Ishmael, which means "God hears," and she called God El Roi, which means "God sees." In the end, He tells her to return and submit to Sarai, and Hagar turns back around.

Their interaction is a beautiful picture of the way Jesus meets us in our most desperate moments. In this passage we get a glimpse of a lonely woman running from her circumstances who has an experience with God that leaves her feeling heard and noticed. That's our God! No matter what you have done, no matter how far you have run, you serve a God who hears you and sees you. No matter how lonely you feel, you are known. The God of Abram is the God of Hagar and the same God of you and me. Again, like an echo of reminder, God shows us that it does not matter where we come from; He loves us in spite of our background, in spite of our decisions and in spite of our circumstances.

A Promise

Genesis 17 takes us even farther in Abram's journey. By now, Abram is 99 years old, and Ishmael is 13. It has been 24 years since God told Abram to leave Haran, and Abram and Sarai have waited for over a decade on God's promise that they would be parents. Then suddenly, God appeared to Abram and proclaimed that He would like to make a covenant with him.

The word for "covenant" used here in chapter 17 is the Hebrew word *berit*, which means "covenant," "treaty" or "agreement."[1] The covenant God makes with Abram in this passage reveals His level of commitment to him—and to us. The Creator of all was seriously committed to this man wandering the earth, and their covenant is a beautiful picture of God's grace, mercy and love.

As a signal of His promise, God gave Abram a new name, Abraham, or "father of a multitude," and reaffirmed His plan to give Abraham and his wife a son named Isaac. Instead of responding with tearful awe, Abraham fell to the ground and laughed in bewilderment that he and Sarah—God gave her a new name, too—could conceive. It gets better. In the following chapter, when Sarah overhears the Lord telling Abraham again that she would bear a child, *she* laughed. No wonder God decided their son would be named Isaac, which means "he laughs." Thankfully, in our moments of foolish unbelief and lack of faith, God is still sovereign, and if He says He will do something, He will do it. As Genesis 18:14 states, "Is anything too hard for the LORD?" We can have confidence that the answer to that question is no.

Abraham's "Here I Am"

All this background brings us to the first "Here I am" statement in Scripture. Beautiful, heaven-sent Isaac was born one year after God established His covenant with Abraham and confirmed that Sarah would bear a son. God proved true, as He always does, and Sarah and Abraham raised their miracle child. Things seem to be going well and then, arriving in Genesis 22, we find the story in which God tells Abraham to sacrifice Isaac.

Verse 1 reads, "After these things God tested Abraham and said to him, 'Abraham!' And he said, 'Here I am.'" We are not told how much time has passed exactly since the last time God spoke to Abraham, but we read here that God called Abraham's name. When He did, immediately Abraham responded, "Here I am."

Before we dive into the meaning of this story, I want to be clear about the first part of the verse: "After these things God tested Abraham." I would not want anyone to walk away with the notion that God is tempting Abraham, and therefore God must be the source of our own temptations. God does not tempt us. James 1:13 says, "Let no one say when he is tempted, 'I am being tempted by God,' for God cannot be tempted with evil, and he himself tempts no one." We see and understand that God does not tempt us. But what He does is test us. There are fundamental differences between tempting and testing. Temptation is a lure to sin; testing develops perseverance and faith. Temptation comes from Satan to condemn; testing comes from God to develop and mature. In this case with Abraham, he is being tested, not tempted. God was not done growing and maturing Abraham, so He brought a test to continue that perfection.

We see from Abraham's quick, affirmative response that he was more than up for the test. It is as if Abraham was eager to hear from the Lord. He was eager to connect and respond to whatever God would desire for him. His immediate, "Here I am," shows an eagerness I hope to have each and every day, and one I pray over you now.

Still, as eager as he may have been, I doubt Abraham was expecting what would come next. So often in his conversations with God over the years there had been promises and covenants abundant. I can picture Abraham excited to hear what new promise God had for him and the good news that was coming his way. I highly doubt he was prepared to hear, "Take your son, your only son Isaac, whom you love, and go to the land of Moriah, and offer him there as a burnt offering on one of the mountains of which I shall tell you" (v. 2).

Can you imagine? Abraham has it all: a wife who loves him, a piece of land to call home, servants and possessions that make him a very wealthy man and, above all, the son and heir he had longed for a son that he gets to train and nurture each day. Isaac, who would have been between fifteen and thirty years old by this time, was certainly Abraham's pride and joy. But instead of a being given a promise, Abraham was told to sacrifice his son.

Perhaps the most powerful part of this story is what happens next. Genesis records that after God spoke to him, Abraham arose early the next morning, prepared for the journey and set off with Isaac. Let's be honest. How many of us would have taken our time getting around to obeying, maybe taking a few days to prepare for the trip? I can imagine stalling as long as possible to soak up those final moments with my loving son. Truth be told, we fall into this trap more than we care to admit. God asks us to do something difficult, and though we agree to obey, we beat around the bush. Remember, however, that

Abraham had learned long before that delayed obedience is still disobedience, and he seems determined not to make the same mistake again. Abraham did not just respond immediately with a verbal, "Here I am," when God called his name; he responded in action as well. What a great directive for us all to follow our words up with action. God said, "Go," and so Abraham went.

Furthermore, Abraham did not even ask God to reconsider His command. It would have been easy to try to rationalize with God, to ask God to spare him from such a thing, to remind Him that Isaac was a promise. But Abraham did not do any of that. God told Abraham to sacrifice his only son, and in the next sentence we see Abraham's immediate obedience.

Can you imagine this? For years you pray for a child, just one son, with your beautiful bride. And finally, after years of trying and crying out to God, your son arrives. You spend years training him in the ways of the Lord and growing close to him. Morning after morning, you wake up to God's promise looking back at you. Then one day, your heavenly Father tells you to sacrifice that son, your greatest treasure. Instead of fighting back, your crying heart musters up enough faith to move forward in obedience.

The thing is, Abraham moved forward immediately, and then he kept moving forward. Three days he journeyed with him, all the while knowing that the son who was following him so willingly, who had trusted him all the days of his life, was about to be bound on an altar by his very hands. It is devastating to think about the anguish Abraham must have carried in his soul. What obedience and courage it took for him to follow God. He is an example to us all.

If Abraham could be ready to say, "Here I am," and offer up his only son, we can be ready to answer God and have the courage to sacrifice our own desires. Charles Spurgeon, in his study of Genesis 22, made this point about our dreams and loves: "Let Isaac be dear, but let Isaac die sooner than God should be distrusted."[2] How convicting, and yet so encouraging. No matter what we have in our life—a dream, a person we love, a promise come true—we must never put those things before God. Even if we believe with all our heart that it is from the Lord, we must never hold it dearer than God. Once it takes that place in our heart, it becomes an idol. Abraham showed that God's precious gift to him had not become an idol and that his priorities were still intact. He was willing to let go of his son in order to hold on to God.

It can be hard to hold loosely the things we love most, but it is exactly what we must do to be a follower of Christ. Jesus is asking each and every one of us to be good stewards of what He has given us but never to hold them so tightly that we are unwilling to let them go.

It is hard, I know. I struggle in significant ways with control. I often feel like if I do not manage what I have and keep it close, I will lose what I care about. Can you relate? Do you too fear you will lose what you care about, so you hold on tighter? If so, I believe God is asking you at this very moment to come to a place where you do not keep those things from Him or idolize what you care about.

Do not forget, Abraham failed at this in the past. But he learned, and through that test he developed the sort of faith that allowed him to trust God with what was most important to him. It was that faith in God that sustained him and gave him the strength to carry out this very challenging task. Hebrews 11:17–19 records:

> By faith Abraham, when he was tested, offered up Isaac, and he who had received the promises was in the act of offering up his only son, of whom it was said, "Through Isaac shall your offspring be named." He considered that God was able even to raise him from the dead, from which, figuratively speaking, he did receive him back.

You see, Abraham remembered the promise that God had given him regarding Isaac. He recalled God's covenant that Isaac would be the son through whom heirs would be established. Therefore, he knew that because God had made a covenant, then He would make good on that, even if He had to raise Isaac from the dead. Abraham's confidence in God's faithfulness was greater than his fear of losing his son.

With much relief we read that God did not allow Abraham to go through with the sacrifice. Just as Abraham was about to strike Isaac, the Lord called out to him. Once again, Abraham answered, "Here I am." The Lord went on to tell Abraham not to sacrifice Isaac but instead to take the ram caught in the nearby thorns and sacrifice it. Isaac was released, and together the father and son made a sacrifice to "the Lord who provides" on Mount Moriah, where the temple would one day stand.

Leaving a Legacy

What we observe from Abraham is faith, obedience and courage. Because of those attributes, God used him to birth a nation. What an incredible testimony!

Can you imagine the impact Abraham's character and faith-filled decisions had on Isaac? Think about it. Isaac knew his father loved him dearly and would do just about anything for him. But he also knew his father loved and followed God, so much that his dad was willing to sacrifice him because God had asked for it. Isaac walked away from that experience on Mount Moriah knowing his father trusted his Father wholeheartedly. That had to have been a huge lesson in faith for Isaac. This was a legacy moment for Abraham—both to Isaac and the nation of Israel. You will also leave a legacy, and you get to decide the nature of it. Will it be a legacy of unbelief, disobedience and fear? Or will it be a legacy of faith, obedience and courage?

I often think about my brother Zach and the legacy he is leaving for his two children. Zach is my younger brother by seven years and one of my best friends. He is the kind of guy people cannot help but like because of his warm and funny personality. You just relax when you are around him, and it is awesome. I may be partial, but the guy is also one of the godliest men I know.

Zach and I did not grow up in a Christian home, and we did not have the best examples when it came to marriage or parenting, especially as it relates to biblical marriage and parenting. Zach and I both approached relationships in a worldly, unhealthy way at times. We just were not equipped for the struggle of temptation nor taught the value of purity. I have already touched on my story, but Zach's is one of incredible grace.

My brother had a serious relationship with a girl he was about to marry at the time. In fact, he had the ring and her father's permission before things fell apart. At a time of great temptation, he and his girlfriend gave in to the flesh and slept together. The week Zach was going to propose, they found out she was pregnant. It is a long and dramatic story, but his girlfriend left him within a few days, and Zach's world was forever changed.

Throughout the pregnancy, Zach had little contact with his ex-girlfriend. However, he did pursue God in a way he never had before. He sought out a mentor who came alongside him and showed him what it meant to be a godly man. He poured over Scripture, read books and prayed consistently. I watched a twenty-year-old man flourish in the presence of God while walking through a season of heartache.

Zach is an example to many. In fact, I often tell him he is my example for parenting. Who knew there was so much to learn from a younger sibling! What is more powerful is the way he modeled what it looks like to persevere through a devastating trial. Zach is someone who made a mistake, sought after the grace and goodness of God and came out on the other end a godly example. He could have given up, become jaded or chosen bitterness, but he did not. He chose obedience to God in the midst of his storm, and as a result, he is leaving a legacy for his son and daughter, for me and for so many who know him. In fact, the man who has mentored him commented on how much he has learned from my brother.

Furthermore, because Zach chose to lean in to God instead of pursuing the flesh during that season of heartbreak, God was able to bring healing to the very relationship that caused him so much pain. After two years, God restored Zach's relationship with his ex-girlfriend, and by the grace of God they are a family of four today. Personally, I think I got the best sister-in-love a girl could ask for.

Chances are, you have a child or children, or perhaps nieces and nephews. I am a mama completely head over heels for a little boy who is one going on eight. Little guy has his mother's determination and independent spirit. But I am also a proud aunt to ten cute little things. I often ask myself, What kind of legacy do I want to pass on to them? When was the last time you asked yourself that question? Think about those behind you who look up to you. You have a unique opportunity to exemplify faith to them. It will be the faith, obedience and courage you show in moments of tests and trials that speak to them and come to their mind when they do not know what to do. I pray with all my heart that when He calls your name, you will be someone who responds immediately—and I mean immediately—in obedience like Abraham.

4

JACOB, THE DECEIVER

The "Here I Am" of Reconciliation

I f there was ever a shady character in the Bible whom God redeemed in a big way, it was Jacob. His name literally means "deceiver," if that tells you anything. Being raised with that name hanging over his head was not always easy, but neither did Jacob always handle it well. It took years of isolation, betrayal and mistakes for him to mature and grow into the kind of man God saw he could be, but God still worked mightily in his life. He saw past Jacob's blunders and used his obedience to bring healing to broken relationships in his family, impacting generations of God's people.

The Bible introduces us to Jacob in Genesis 25. It is perhaps the most interesting birth besides Jesus' in the Bible. His entry into the world is indicative of struggle to come and sets the stage for this story of a family divided. Intrigued? Good!

Isaac and Rebekah were barren for many years, much like Isaac's own parents, but at last the Lord opened Rebekah's womb and allowed her to conceive. She did notice some struggle within her during pregnancy, and when she inquired of the Lord as to why, He told her there were two babies within her.

> Two nations are in your womb, and two peoples from within you shall be divided; the one shall be stronger than the other, the older shall serve the younger.
>
> Genesis 25:23

Jacob came out of his mother's womb clasping at the heel of his twin brother, Esau. This made Esau the oldest and heir to the family birthright and blessing. From the very beginning, tension stewed and a family was at odds.

A Family Divided

After the birth of the boys, the Bible jumps years ahead. Esau grew into the more skilled hunter, while Jacob was often at home tending to the needs there. They were as different as could be. One day Esau returned home from hunting in the wilderness and was starving. When he walked into the warm house, Jacob was making stew, and Esau pleaded with him for a bowl.

Now, this is where we begin to see how Jacob got his reputation for being a deceiver. In response to his brother's request for food, Jacob attempted to negotiate a deal—a deal Jacob had no doubt planned to make for a while. It seems he was just waiting for the right moment to secure the birthright belonging to his brother. That birthright, which was given to the firstborn son, granted Esau a double-portion inheritance and established his role as the family priest. Amazingly, Esau agreed to exchange his birthright for a bowl of stew. Friend, never make a decision when you are hangry, okay?

Aside from the fact that Esau made a dumb move, Jacob showed pretty lousy character here. The guy was willing to let his twin brother starve over a birthright—something that belonged to Esau—and leveraged Esau's discomfort to manipulate him.

It gets worse.

As the boys' father, Isaac, wasted away on his deathbed, Rebekah, their mother, concocted a scheme to trick Isaac into giving the blessing reserved for the firstborn son to Jacob instead of Esau. This blessing would have granted Esau prosperity and the covenant line. Jacob did briefly resist the idea, but in the end he gave in and chose to deceive his father and cheat his brother. He dressed up like Esau in order to lie to his father, whose poor eyesight and failing senses prevented him from discerning the truth. Furthermore, Jacob used God as part of his alibi to sell the lie. Talk about a soap opera.

The truth is, God had already promised the birthright and blessing to Jacob. He did not need to steal it. But he did, and by taking matters into his own hands, he suffered unimaginable hurt. Jacob's deceit that night became a web of lies that eventually left him bound and robbed him of so much. When Esau learned of the deception, he was understandably infuriated and planned to kill Jacob after the death of their father. Rightly, Jacob feared for his life, and at his mother's urging, he fled. Jacob never saw his mother again and lived in exile for many years. Little did he know that his deep pain would pave the way for God to enter Jacob's life powerfully and begin to work an incredible transformation.

The Tables Turned

Jacob's exile from his homeland began a journey that would forever change his life. It was a journey that would take him all the way to Haran, the land of his mother's family.

I cannot imagine how hard that first night was for him. Jacob set up camp in the wilderness, where a hard rock was his pillow.

I bet the weight of what just happened came tumbling down on him like a tidal wave, his thoughts and emotions spilling over and nearly drowning him in a moment of authentic realization. Jacob was indeed alone, on the run, and finally, deeply feeling the ramifications of what he had just done. The rift he had created in his family could not be undone. His selfish act of manipulation now had a cost that came calling.

As he nestled into that rock and drifted off with only a blanket of pain and hurt to keep him warm, Jacob had no clue what was about to happen next: God was going to enter the scene and meet him at his rock bottom. Jacob had a dream that night that served as his first encounter with the Lord God Almighty. No doubt, that dream was what he had always hoped for in his endeavor to be known and important. In fact, it confirmed his place in history.

That night in Jacob's dream, God appeared to him and made a promise to him confirming a very important covenant. God told Jacob that descendants as numerous as the dust of the earth would come from him and that the very land Jacob now slept on would be an inheritance for his family. But that is not all. God promised that He would be with Jacob and protect him, that He would keep him safe all his days and one day bring Jacob back home.

For a man alone and on the run, those must have been sweet words to his wounded heart. What a comfort and joy this must have been for Jacob! I can only imagine it was this promise and source of hope that carried him through the lonely and heavy days to come. From where I sit, that is a whole lot of grace for a guy who just made a royal mess.

I want to get to Jacob's "Here I am" moment, so let's briefly go over the next few decades of his life. Jacob did make it to Haran and was welcomed with open arms by his Uncle Laban. He then fell in love with Laban's youngest daughter, Rachel. To marry her, he agreed to work for his uncle for seven years.

So Jacob worked the seven years. This is where the deceiver was deceived! That night, instead of bringing Rachel to Jacob, Laban brought Leah, the older sister. It is believed that Jacob did not recognize the difference because he was drunk. Whatever the reason, it was not until the next morning he realized he had married the wrong woman! Laban agreed to give Rachel to Jacob in exchange for another seven years of work, which Jacob honored. Over the years, sister rivalry ensued, children were born and family drama reached an all-time high.

I cannot help but wonder if being on the other end of deceit was necessary for Jacob's transformation process. Perhaps he had to experience firsthand what he had dealt out and to feel the full weight of it. Knowing the heartache it caused perhaps allowed Jacob to empathize with Esau and help Jacob to let go of that part of his identity.

The remaining formation of Jacob's new identity took place on his way back home. After working for Laban for many years, growing a family and acquiring great wealth, Jacob finally got the go-ahead from God to make his journey home. Jacob had matured and changed, and it was time to face his brother.

Jacob's First "Here I Am"

Jacob had two "Here I am" moments in his long life. His first one took place in a dream during a time when dissension was stirring with Laban's family. Here's the moment, as recorded in Genesis 31:11–13 (emphasis added):

> Then the angel of God said to me in the dream, "Jacob," and I said, "Here I am!" And he said . . . "I have seen all that Laban is doing to you. I am the God of Bethel, where you anointed a pillar and made a vow to me. Now *arise, go out from this land and return to the land of your kindred.*"

Jacob had built himself a cushy life in Haran. He had a large family, great wealth and security. Back home did not hold the same comfort and assurance; back home held fear and uncertainty. But God was ready to take Jacob on a new journey and to a new place spiritually. After years of life lived hard, Jacob had matured and learned to tune in to the voice of God. More importantly, he was now in a place where he could say, "Here I am," when God called his name.

In the dream, God instructed Jacob to return home to Esau and the land of his youth, to leave the comfortable for the unknown. But, as we will see soon, God was calling Jacob from his cushy life so that reconciliation could take place. It is this step of obedience that would restore a family.

And obey Jacob did. He packed up his large family and started the journey home as a result of his first "Here I am."

A Name Change

What happened on Jacob's journey home is one of my favorite stories in the Bible. When Jacob was nearing home, he sent messengers ahead to let Esau know he was returning. When the messengers came back, they informed Jacob that Esau was on his way with four hundred men. Jacob was no doubt scared. Last he heard, Esau wanted to kill him. Jacob did the only thing left to do: pray.

> Then Jacob prayed, "O God of my father Abraham, God of my father Isaac, LORD, you who said to me, 'Go back to your country and your relatives, and I will make you prosper,' I am unworthy of all the kindness and faithfulness you have shown your servant. I had only my staff when I crossed this Jordan, but now I have become two camps. Save me, I pray, from the hand of my brother Esau, for I am afraid he will come and attack me, and also the mothers with their children. But you have said, 'I

will surely make you prosper and will make your descendants
like the sand of the sea, which cannot be counted.'"

Genesis 32:9–12 NIV

I am so moved by Jacob's humility and dependence on God.
There was a time He would have taken matters into his own
hands, even though God had already said He would take care
of it. Old Jacob likely would have gathered all the men and prepared for a fight. But new Jacob had a new heart and a different
idea. He prayed before doing anything. He humbled himself
before God and asked for protection. Furthermore, he sent a
gift ahead to meet Esau to show his brother honor.

The night he prayed that prayer was the moment that forever
changed Jacob, and I am so glad it is in the Bible. Jacob was
about to become who God always knew he could be.

That night Jacob camped alone and was met by a stranger,
who was an angel of the Lord. They wrestled—all night. At
daybreak, when the angel realized Jacob would not let go, he
touched Jacob's hip and left him with a limp. Still, Jacob did
not let go. Genesis 32:26 (NIV) tells us, "Jacob replied, 'I will
not let you go unless you bless me.'" Jacob was not going to
give up. No, Jacob wanted God's blessing, and he was not stopping until he got it. At one time he would have manipulated
his circumstances for it, but now he was willing to go to God
Himself and wrestle Him until he got it.

In response to his request, God asked Jacob what his name
was. He answered, "Jacob." It may seem a benign-enough exchange, but this was a pivotal moment in Jacob's transformation. It was the turning point. God was asking about more than
his name. His question was about Jacob's identity. God wanted
Jacob to acknowledge what kind of man he had been all those
years so he could move beyond it and embrace the new man
he was becoming. He was saying he could no longer be known
as a heel grabber, looking for opportunities to get ahead and

manipulate others. He must now assume his place not as Jacob but as Israel.

Israel means "he struggles with God," and that was certainly what Jacob had done. He had wrestled with God for a blessing, which he got—and more! Jacob returned home to a welcoming Esau, praise God. God honored Jacob's willingness to rise to the occasion by bringing reconciliation and restoration to the broken relationships in his past.

Have you ever found yourself wrestling with God? I read this account and cannot help but see myself in it. After being in the Christian workforce for fourteen years now, I have stepped out and into a new season, a season that is harder than I ever imagined. I have transitioned from work to being home with my son and writing full-time from there. It is something I had hoped to do for a long time, but it has its challenges. For instance, sometimes I wonder if I am taking a step back instead of moving forward. I have always been a driven person and a high achiever, but here, at home, nobody notices me in this hiddenness. There is no promotion or accolade for a job well done. This process is certainly doing something to my character. Like Jacob wrestling with the Lord for a blessing and finding his new self under the cloak of the dark night, I feel myself wrestling with God about who I am and what is ahead. I do not want to let go of the wrestle, either, until I have secured His blessing. I am ready for a name change.

The thing about that goal is that it takes a whole lot of smaller seasons of failure, missteps, some minor successes and refinement. Jacob went through so much loss as a result of his poor choices but also found success along the way. It was this kind of trial and error that forged the man who would go from Jacob to Israel. It is the same thing we must submit to if we too want a new name and identity in Christ.

Every season has purpose, and God uses it all—even the messy—for good. I point this out because part of getting to the place where you can hear God's voice and say, "Here I am," is the journey of ups and downs. Every single person we highlight in this book failed multiple times along the way. They all made mistakes and experienced disappointment in their stories. Getting to their "Here I am" moment meant failing along the way and allowing those failures to make them more like Jesus.

Are you in a season of wrestling, determined to come out more like Him? Are you seeing your own struggles make you better? Or do you need to gain that determination, like Jacob did? Ask yourself, Are you willing to fight, to lose part of yourself, in order to become who He wants you to be? Remember, just as God was faithful to Jacob to form him into the person and for the purpose He ordained, God will not leave you. He will meet you where you are, and He will make you new.

Jacob's Second "Here I Am"

In the years after Israel's reconciliation with Esau, he lost his father, Isaac, and his wife Rachel. His twelve sons grew up, but not everything went well among them. Most turned against Joseph, one of the younger sons, and sold him into slavery in Egypt. Joseph was Israel's favorite son, so this loss hit him like a dagger to the heart. He thought his son was dead when, in fact, Joseph's own journey was just starting. He would go from slave to prisoner to second-in-command of Egypt. While Joseph was in leadership, a famine hit Canaan, where Israel (formerly Jacob, remember!) and his family were living. This is where we pick back up.

Through a series of events, Joseph's brothers came to Egypt to ask for life-saving rations of food and water, and they ended up making their plea before Joseph, not knowing it was him. In time, Joseph revealed himself as their brother and extended forgiveness to them. Instead of merely giving them the provisions they came for, he asked his brothers to go back home to gather their families, including Israel, and return to Egypt to live, where they would no longer have to suffer from the famine in their land. When Israel heard the good news, he was no doubt overwhelmed with joy. He packed everything up and quickly set out on the journey to be with Joseph in Egypt.

Let's be honest for a moment. Even though Israel was excited to see Joseph, leaving Canaan was not exactly easy. It was the Promised Land, his inheritance. It was the place God had given to him for his descendants. To leave without assurance of a return—even if leaving meant being reunited with Joseph and refuge from the famine—was still a step of faith. Israel had to trust God that everything would eventually come together.

Along the way the caravan stopped overnight, and Israel had his second "Here I am" moment.

> And God spoke to Israel in visions of the night and said, "Jacob, Jacob." And he said, "Here I am." Then he said, "I am God, the God of your father. Do not be afraid to go down to Egypt, for there I will make you into a great nation. I myself will go down with you to Egypt, and I will also bring you up again, and Joseph's hand shall close your eyes."
>
> Genesis 46:2–4

These words were a confirmation of the path Israel was on and contained a promise. His family would once again be restored as Israel stepped out into the great unknown, and in his old age Israel would be granted a great blessing—to die among all of his sons.

Israel's decision to allow God to work in him and his ability to tune in to God's voice afforded him the great blessings of individual and generational healing. Both of his "Here I am" moments brought about restoration in his life and in his family. After the first, he was reconciled with his only brother, his twin.

After the second, he was reunited with a son he thought was gone forever. Can you imagine how beautiful those reunions must have been for him? It is even sweeter when you consider that these were gifts God lavished on a man who once left hurt and broken spirits in his wake through deceit and manipulation. Can we just take a moment and declare how great our God is!

Like Israel, you will find healing when you are willing to say, "Here I am," and step out of your comfort zone into the unknown in pursuit of obedience to God. The journey that follows will chip away at your old self and forge a new person, one able to let go of what is comfortable for the promise of something better. Only through that journey, when you are free from what holds you back, can God mend your heart, as he did Israel's.

Where do you need healing? Whom are you praying to find reconciliation with? To find your way to this kind of reconciliation, you will need to step out in faith. It may seem overwhelming, but if you will take the road carved out by the mighty hands of God, you will no doubt find the answer to your prayer.

5

MOSES, THE LEADER

The "Here I Am" That Breaks Strongholds

Have you ever been riddled with insecurity to the point of debilitation? Yeah, me too. Lots! I do not say that with a positive excitement but rather as an affirmation of shared experience. It is to let you know I have been there and that we might get each other.

I was plagued with insecurities so heavy they dictated how (little) I valued myself in my teen years. It probably took off in junior high when, as a result of having fair skin and dark hair, I was nicknamed Marilyn Manson after the infamous heavy metal artist popular at the time. Not the kind of perception you want as a preteen girl. I used to be so afraid of what people thought about me in high school that I was nervous even to walk across the cafeteria during lunch. I was a quiet introvert living in my head and dreaming to be someone more confident. I wanted to be someone else.

Thankfully, I became a Christian as a junior in high school, and being in a godly environment at church, surrounded by people who were nonjudgmental and nurturing, allowed me to come out of my shell and celebrate who God created me to be. I flourished in a safe community filled with people who wanted to know me.

Now, I still had—and have—my moments of self-doubt. For years I struggled with an insecurity about the pitch of my speaking voice. When I was a young thing in ministry, I often had the opportunity to be in videos at the church. After I had gained some significant experience in those videos, someone suggested I might do well with voice-overs, so I was brought in to record my voice. The guy recording was a friend and jokingly said after I was done that I sounded like a twelve-year-old girl and he would not use my recordings. I did great on video because you could see I was an adult, he teased, but it did not translate here. From then on, I was self-conscious about my high-pitched voice, even when you could see my face.

When God called me to launch a podcast roughly ten years later, I was hesitant. I was so concerned with what people would think about my voice and was sure nobody would listen. But I decided to be obedient to His call, and I am so thankful I was, because now thousands are tuning in to hear how God has redeemed people's stories. I could have stayed curled up in a cocoon and missed what God wanted to do, but instead, I trusted God with that insecurity, and it has allowed me to point people to Him. Now when that fear—or another—tries to hold me captive and keep me from being obedient to the call of God on my life, I refuse to listen to its whispers. I listen to one voice, and that is the Father's.

Moses was a man riddled with insecurity as well. Even though he had the best education and everything he could ever want at his fingertips, he was still just a man who struggled with confidence in his ability to effect much change, let alone lead. And yet, when God was ready to make good on

His promise to Abraham to bring Israel out of captivity and into the Promised Land, Moses was the guy He had in sight for such a task.

A little background on Moses' upbringing: After Joseph's family settled in the land, the Israelites grew to great numbers—so great that around the time that Moses was born, the pharaoh issued an edict that all firstborn males should be killed to help with population control of the Hebrews. In a last-ditch effort to save his life, Moses' family placed him in a waterproofed basket and floated him out into the river. It just so happened that the basket with baby Moses in it was discovered by the pharaoh's daughter, who took Moses home and raised him, a Hebrew baby, as her own son in the pharaoh's house in Egypt.

I am not quite sure where the insecurities began for him. Perhaps it was being abandoned as an infant and growing up in a palace surrounded by people of a different culture who had royal blood. Maybe it was the speech impediment we know he dealt with. Whatever the source of Moses' lack of confidence, it was compounded when at the age of forty he exiled himself from Egypt after killing an Egyptian who was beating a Hebrew slave. Shunned by both Hebrews and Egyptians, Moses fled into the desert, where he spent the next forty years as a shepherd. In fact, it was there in his exile in the wilderness that Moses had his "Here I am" moment. But let's focus on the desert first.

Forged in the Desert

The desert seasons in our lives make great furnaces of transformation. A desert fire burns out the insecurities in our lives, and a confidence in God is fanned into flame. In the heat and drought and isolation from others, we come out more like

Christ. Though painful, these seasons can be a great conduit for maturity. That was certainly the case for Moses.

Moses spent forty years in the Egyptian culture, and it brought him to murder. I find it quite interesting that when he pulled away from Egypt, it took another forty years before God called him to the great purpose for which he was born. My conclusion is this: Because Moses had forty years of the world in him, God needed forty years in the wilderness to pull out the guilt, shame, brokenness and baggage. The desert was a pruning ground for him and a place to draw near to the God he had not known for so many years. Moses had so much to learn about himself and the character of the Father.

Being in the desert is never fun. Moses often lived in solitude as he led his flock across the lonely land. While he had grown up being catered to, he now sacrificed comfort for the care of his sheep. He was once someone with great power and influence, and now he lived in obscurity. But it was only here could he be stripped of the old Moses and molded into the kind of godly man who could lead thousands out of slavery.

Maybe you are in the midst of your own desert experience right now, and Moses' story hits a little too close to home. If you find yourself feeling alone, forgotten and without purpose, or if the pain you are going through seems so great you simply want to give up, I want to remind you of this: The desert has value. It probably hurts like the dickens and causes you to want to throw your arms into the air in defeat, but it has value. Trust me when I say that your desert has more promise than any mountaintop experience.

Your desert is a place to foster character, intimacy and dreams like nothing else in this world can produce. If you will lean into this season, God will do the work in you that must be done before stepping into a dream that only the desert can forge. When the journey gets tough, listen closely and you will hear God whispering these precious words to your spirit:

I have not forgotten you. I know you and love you. It's because I know you and love you that I have brought you through the trials and into the desert. You have so much in you that I want to pull out. It has not been easy, and it's not over, but I bring you through these trials to refine you, to make you more like Me. I do this because I love you and have great plans for you that cannot include those things from the past. I have you, and you are not forgotten. Trust Me, child.

Like Moses, your desert season—if you persevere—will catapult you forward into the ultimate plan and purpose God has for your life. Will you lean into Him? Will you allow the desert to mold a person God wants to use for great things in the Kingdom?

Doubting the Call

Like I said at the beginning of this book, in order to answer the unique call of God on your life, you must first develop the ability to distinguish His voice above all the other voices in this world. It is perhaps equally problematic and wonderful that God calls to each of us differently. For Abraham, conversation with God was regular enough that God could appear at any moment and pick up a conversation with him, like old friends. For Jacob, it was always in a dream. As we will see, over and over again God used signs to speak to, speak through and to strengthen Moses.

In fact, Moses' "Here I am" moment began with a sign in the wilderness, far from the loud surroundings where he grew up. As we have seen, Moses had to make some mistakes, wrestle with his identity and submit to forty years of pruning in the isolated wilderness to get to the point where he could hear God's voice. I doubt Moses knew what was happening when God decided his time of preparation had ended.

For all we know, it began as any normal day out shepherding the flock that belonged to his father-in-law. Moses was on the far side of the wilderness at the mountain of God called Horeb, and as he was there, a bush set fire. But the bush did not burn up; it kept a flame. Curious, Moses approached the bush.

> When the LORD saw that he had gone over to look, God called to him from within the bush, "Moses! Moses!" And Moses said, "Here I am."
>
> Exodus 3:4 NIV

Can we just stop and reflect on this for a moment? There is no record of God talking to Moses before this moment. For all we know, this was the first time he had heard from the Lord. In fact, it is likely that this was the first time, as in the following verses God describes who He is and mentions not to be afraid.

Surprisingly, Moses took the encounter fairly calmly—so calmly that he had the presence of mind in the moment to argue with God. Now, I doubt Moses was trying to be argumentative. His objections were rooted in his significant insecurities, which allowed doubt to cloud his mind and judgment to such a degree that no less than five times in this conversation Moses questioned God regarding the call on his life. Yet, God did not chastise him or take away the opportunity. This should lend great relief to us in our doubts. If God was patient with Moses—even when Moses tested His patience to the limit—He will be patient with us.

Doubt One

From the midst of the burning bush, God began the conversation by telling Moses He would send him to Egypt to deliver the people of Israel from the oppression inflicted by Pharaoh. Remember, Pharaoh was a guy Moses was once related to and was likely close to. God was sending the only Hebrew who knew Pharaoh personally to him to set the captives free. Yet Moses immediately questioned his qualifications for such a significant task. He replied, "Who am I that I should go to Pharaoh and bring the Israelites out of Egypt?" (Exodus 3:11 NIV).

The truth is, God had been preparing Moses for this moment from his birth. Without God's intervention in his life, Moses could not have hoped to get an audience with Pharaoh. But God was not asking Moses to handle any of the planning. All He required was Moses' willingness.

All He requires from you is your willingness. It is possible you are neither perfectly qualified nor the best person for the job God has called you to, but if He has indeed called you, He will equip you. Trust Him to take care of all the details. He is not asking you to be one hundred percent ready; He is asking you to be one hundred percent faithful to the call.

On the other hand, it seems possible that Moses' objection was an expression of misplaced humility. Moses had to know that no other Hebrew was connected to Pharaoh like he was, and he was trained to be a leader. Surely, deep down, he knew he was the most obvious choice for the job. While in his younger days he might have felt immediately honored that God sought him out for such an important task, his time in the desert had humbled him. Perhaps he worried that acknowledging his impressive qualifications would be prideful rather than a mere statement of fact. Sometimes in the process of laying aside our pride we can develop the false idea that thinking less of ourselves is humility. When God is asking you to step out, it is not humility to question your contribution; it is doubt— a doubt of your value and worth and, ultimately, a doubt of God's plan.

Doubt Two

In spite of God's reassurance that He would be with Moses, Moses still responded with doubt: "Suppose I go to the Israelites and say to them, 'The God of your fathers has sent me to you,' and they ask me, 'What is his name?' Then what shall I tell them?" (Exodus 3:13 NIV).

After forty years away from his people—and after spending the previous forty living in an Egyptian household—Moses doubted that he knew enough about God to persuade leaders of Israel to listen to him. Surely the Hebrews would want some sort of validation that God Almighty had called him to free Israel, but how could Moses prove he did, indeed, know God when he was not even sure what he should call Him?

To counteract Moses' doubt in his ability to sound spiritual enough to impress the Hebrew leaders, God revealed Himself in a brand-new way. He told Moses to tell the people that "I AM WHO I AM" had sent him (v. 14 NIV). This was the mic drop of names. Instead of identifying Himself as "the LORD, the God of your fathers—the God of Abraham, Isaac and Jacob" (v. 16 NIV), which only referenced His connection to past leaders, this new name established that God was going to work through Moses now.

Instead of shining a light on what Moses could—or could not—recite from the history books, this new name demonstrated that God was writing a brand-new story through His servant. It did not matter if Moses was too Egyptian for the Hebrews, too Hebrew for the Egyptians, or if he had spent too long in the desert to relate to either of those groups. God had revealed Himself to Moses as the One who was and is and is to come—the great I AM. "This," God told Moses to tell the Hebrew leaders, "is my name forever, the name you shall call me from generation to generation" (v. 15 NIV).

Doubt Three

God went on to reveal His plan and Moses' place in it. Not only would He free the Israelites from captivity, but He would orchestrate their exodus in such a way that His people would leave Egypt with gold in their pockets.

Nonetheless, at the first opportunity to get a word in, Moses wondered aloud once again how a lowly shepherd could make a difference: "What if they do not believe me or listen to me and say, 'The LORD did not appear to you'?" (Exodus 4:1 NIV). In spite of all God's plans and promises, Moses doubted God's call. There, faced with a miracle and hearing the audible voice of God, Moses allowed insecurity to dictate his response.

Instead of announcing, "Three doubts and you're out!" God's answer to Moses shows the depth of His grace and patience and reflects His desire for Moses—and for us—to trust Him absolutely. If His plans and promises were not sufficient to overcome the whispers of doubt and insecurity that plagued Moses, God would speak to His servant through another means: signs and miracles that visually demonstrated the power that Moses would yield in God's name. To build his confidence there on the spot, God allowed Moses to see and practice the three signs He would perform before Pharaoh.

Sadly, the signs were still not enough. Moses doubted again.

Doubts Four and Five

I do not know about you, but my heart swells with faith and awe as I read this exchange between God and Moses. Imagine what it would be like to stand in front of a miracle-in-progress and hear the audible voice of God telling you which way to go and what to do. What if every major decision unfolded like this? It seems like it would be a much easier way to live and serve Him, doesn't it?

But in real time, life does not always unfold the way it looks on paper. It is easy to imagine what we would do in Moses' shoes—or even to judge him for his response—from the comfort of twenty-first-century perspective. We know how the story ended. We know God came through for Moses, because it is our history. We can turn up our noses at Moses' struggle to trust God because we are not the ones wrestling against decades of insecurity and fear. For Moses, in the moment, this call was totally overwhelming. It meant trusting God to use him for the seemingly impossible task of freeing the Hebrews from slavery, but it also required that Moses address the strongholds of insecurity and doubt in his life.

At this point in the conversation, Moses still was not ready or able to do that. He politely interjects once again, this time revealing another insecurity: "Pardon your servant, Lord. I have never been eloquent, neither in the past nor since you have spoken to your servant. I am slow of speech and tongue" (Exodus 4:10 NIV). Moses did not believe he could be a leader because he lacked a certain eloquence he assumed he needed to be useful. But God said differently.

> The LORD said to him, "Who gave human beings their mouths? Who makes them deaf or mute? Who gives them sight or makes them blind? Is it not I, the LORD? Now go; I will help you speak and will teach you what to say."
>
> vv. 11–12 NIV

When Moses yet again doubted his ability, God reminded him who is in control. Who the Creator is. Who really has the power. God was pointing to an observable example from Moses' own experience that demonstrated He was powerful enough not only to call him but also to equip him fully.

This time Moses did not question God. He just straight out asked God to send someone else. It did not matter to Moses that

God had responded to all his doubts. It did not calm his fears or silence his insecurities when God detailed how He would provide and take care of the situation. Even three separate miracles could not help Moses tip the balance of faith and fear in favor of trusting God. This, friends, is a picture of bondage, and it is not pretty.

That is when God's anger burned against Moses. In a final, frustrated attempt to calm Moses' lingering doubts, He offered to bring in Moses' brother, Aaron, as a voice in the great exodus to come. God would still speak only to Moses, but Moses would be allowed to use Aaron as his mouthpiece. That did the trick. Only a few verses later, we find Moses on the journey back to Egypt.

Keep Saying Yes

It is amazing what can happen when you decide to listen to who God says you are and push past the insecurities that have held you in bondage. When you decide to step into the plan God has for you instead of resisting it because you lack confidence in your value, your life—and others'—will never be the same.

There, standing in front of the burning bush and then again with every step toward Egypt, Moses did just that. In spite of some hesitancy, he turned his insecurities and fears over to the Lord over and over again, and as a result God was able to use him to lead Israel out of captivity. God did what He said He would do, both in Moses and through Himself.

Moses' response provides a valuable lesson. As important as saying "Here I am" is to your journey, it is not enough. You must be willing to say yes continually to the call of God on your life. After your first step forward in obedience, you must keep walking, even if you are packed full of insecurities. And in all likelihood, the insecurities will not go away simply because you overcame them once. But just as God honored His promises to Moses and remained with him through every step of his journey, God will be with you. He will fight for you. He will comfort you. He will transform you, and He will be able to change others' lives because of your obedience.

Breaking Strongholds

God was gracious with Moses' doubts, and He did incredible things through him, but the Scriptures tell us God had even greater things in store. Though he overcame many of his fears, Moses' persistent doubts and insecurities put a cap on how far he would go. In the end, in spite of the awe-inspiring miracles he performed and the freedom he brought to God's people, Moses still fell short of what was possible. What a sobering thought.

Could insecurity be holding you back from stepping into the call of God on your life? Into what area of your life is the enemy inserting doubt? Is it in your intelligence? *Well, I didn't go to college, and I'm certainly not as smart as so-and-so. God surely needs someone more like her.* Is it in your past? *I didn't grow up a Christian and have a lot to learn before God can work through me.* Or, *I have made so many mistakes; how could God use someone with my past to make a difference?* Is it because someone has spoken hurtful words over you? *They said I wasn't good enough and didn't have any value to benefit others, so God could not use me.*

For me, social media is a significant trigger. Sometimes I hop on as I write, and if I am not careful, I can quickly fall into the trap of downing myself as I see more successful writers. But you know what? My Instagram likes and follower count do not represent my value in the Kingdom and how far God wants to use me. Can I get an amen!

As real as these insecurities are and as raw as the emotions can be, they are still lies. They are strongholds the enemy will use to lock you into ineffectiveness for the Kingdom. Recognizing this and identifying your specific doubts are the first steps to freedom. Take those steps and then keep walking.

You have a decision today and every day moving forward: Are you going to believe the lie and remain inactive, paralyzed by fear? Or are you going to listen to what God says about you and step into the call He has placed on your life? Let's commit to each other right now to do the latter!

6

SAMUEL, THE JUDGE

The "Here I Am" That Obeys God's Voice

I t is good for the aching soul to read about godly men and women in the Bible who messed up big time like we do and were still used by God. It makes us feel less like a hot mess and more like redemption is possible. But sometimes it is refreshing to read about the unwavering, too. They serve as beautiful examples that we do not have to keep repeating the same old mistakes and turning over the same struggles, that trusting God and walking faithfully in our calling is possible. Samuel is one of those people, and truly, every time I read about him, I am so encouraged and refreshed. Samuel is my absolute favorite person in the whole Bible and one of the best examples we have in the Scriptures of faithfulness.

To really get a good feel for who Samuel was, we must back up a bit and explore the life of his mother, Hannah. In 1 Samuel 1 we read that Hannah was married to a man named Elkanah, but she was not his only wife. In fact, Elkanah had two wives, and the other was named Peninnah. The Bible tells us that Peninnah had children but Hannah did not.

Hannah was greatly troubled that she was barren. If you are a woman who has ever wanted a child, you can imagine how hard this was for her. Hannah longed for a child in her arms, and in spite of Elkanah's love for Hannah, her barrenness likely caused her to question her worth. It did not help that her husband's other wife constantly pushed that emotional button. If it was not already hard enough that Hannah could not have what she desired most, a son, Peninnah often taunted her and made her feel worse about her struggle.

The Scriptures tell us that Elkanah would often go to the temple with his family to worship the Lord. Hannah went heavy and burdened, time and again. On one particular occasion, Hannah was greatly distressed and, with sobs of pain, cried out to God to give her a child. She vowed that if God would open her womb, she would give the child back to Him. The priest, Eli, was nearby as Hannah prayed fervently. As he witnessed her prayer, he actually thought she was drunk. When he confronted her and learned she was instead greatly distressed, he prayed that God would grant her what she prayed for.

God heard Hannah's prayer that day, and when she returned home, she did indeed conceive a son, whom she named Samuel. She raised him until he was weaned, and then she did what she promised God she would do—she gave him back to the Lord. When the time came, Hannah took Samuel to the temple and gave him to Eli to serve in the Lord's house.

Can we pause for a moment and really soak this in? So often we promise God everything in our distress: "God, if You would only do this, I will do anything for You!" Yet, when He answers, we forget His faithfulness and go back on our commitment to Him. Hannah, however, prayed for a child and promised to give the child back, and guess what? She was faithful to her promise. Hannah could have so easily held Samuel in her arms and changed her mind. Any parent knows that giving up a child would be the hardest thing in the world, and that reality could have made Hannah go back on her word. But she did not. She did what she promised the Lord, no matter how hard it was.

What have you committed to the Lord? Have you followed through on your promise, or are you hesitant because the task seems too difficult? If being faithful to your word seems too challenging, remember Hannah, and let her obedience prompt you to be obedient as well. What she did was incredibly hard, but because of her faithfulness, a dedicated and godly priest was given to the nation of Israel. Samuel was a man who would lead well and go on to mentor the great King David. Hannah's yes was a gift to the world.

Samuel's "Here I Am"

Samuel's "Here I am" moment took place when he was around the age of eleven, according to the Jewish historian Josephus. He was a child and the youngest of all the men who uttered this phrase, but already Samuel had cultivated a spirit that God could speak to. And He did indeed speak.

First Samuel 3 picks up Samuel's story at this age and begins by reminding us that Samuel was living in the temple under the care of Eli, the priest. It also tells us that "the word of the LORD was rare in those days" (v. 1), which means God had been silent. It does not mean He was not working, because He was. God was orchestrating every detail up to this point. Silence does not equate stagnation—not in history, and not in your life. Even though God may seem distant, it does not mean He is not working.

The Bible says that when Samuel's moment took place, he was sleeping next to the ark of the Lord. I love this because it shows the kind of hunger and curiosity Samuel had for God at such a young age. He wanted to be as close to the presence of God as he could, even as he slept. God was the center of his world, and he was determined to serve Him in every moment of the day.

Let me ask you: Do you crave the presence of God? Are you hungry for Him? It is worth noting that if you are longing to hear from God, you must get into His presence as much as possible and pursue closeness with Him. You are promised in Scripture that when you draw near to God, He will draw near to you. Do not overlook the importance of spending time with the Father and cultivating intimacy through intentional pursuit and service.

Samuel's desire for God's presence yielded a significant return. That night, while he was sleeping near the ark, God called his name: "Then the LORD called Samuel, and he said, 'Here I am!'" (1 Samuel 3:4). Assuming it was the elderly priest who called his name in the night, Samuel went to Eli to see what he needed, only to be sent back to bed. God called Samuel's name two more times, and each time the boy went to Eli. It was not until the third time Samuel came into his room that Eli realized what may have been happening and instructed Samuel to respond to the Lord.

This time, after Samuel responded, God continued speaking. He told Samuel that Eli's sons, who were serving as priests in the temple, had been disobedient and that because Eli knew this and did not do anything about it, Eli's house would be punished. What Samuel heard was not good news, and it was not necessarily a prompt for Samuel to do anything; it was God sharing His plan and communicating to Samuel he would be the voice of God to Israel.

When Eli asked the next morning what God had spoken, Samuel told the truth, and Eli knew it. It was no surprise to the priest what God had said, and he knew it was righteous.

From this point on, all of Israel knew Samuel would be God's voice to the nation.

The Fruit of Samuel's "Here I Am"

Honestly, it would take its own book to talk about all of Samuel's accomplishments over the years and his faithful service to God and His people. First Samuel 3:19 says that after his first exchange with the Lord, "Samuel grew, and the LORD was with him and let none of his words fall to the ground." He ended up assuming the role of head priest over Israel.

Before kings ruled, the priest led, because he heard the voice of God. This made the priest head honcho. But over time, the people of Israel became preoccupied with how all the other countries operated and wanted to be more like them, including having a king. God's system of government, where He would lead and take care of them, was not enough for them, and in their shortsightedness, they asked Samuel for a king, a man they could follow. When Samuel brought this before the Lord, God spoke to him to give the people what they wanted. This was not about Samuel, God told him, but about the people's rejection of Him. And so, the journey to appoint Saul, the first king, began.

When Saul took the throne as the first king of Israel, he was not a selfish person out to do wrong. Over time, however, he allowed pride to corrupt his heart, and eventually he pulled away from God. Samuel was the one to clean up after Saul's mistakes, providing counsel, guidance and even correction.

Let's take 1 Samuel 15, for example. God had commanded Saul and his army not only to defeat the Amalekites but to completely wipe them out—as in, leave no survivors; not even one. Instead, out of a fear of his men, Saul spared the Amalekite king and their best livestock. When Samuel heard this, he was beside himself. Scripture says that Samuel cried out to the Lord for an entire night in his grief over the disobedience of Saul and what it meant for the kingdom.

The next day, Samuel confronted Saul and called out his disobedience. Then Samuel killed the Amalekite king, carrying out God's will himself where Saul had failed. After that day, Samuel did not see Saul again until the day of the king's death. However, in the meantime, he anointed a new king to rule after Saul, David.

In a time of great transition for the wandering nation of Israel, Samuel's eagerness to serve allowed him to be a clear and steady voice of truth. From his "Here I am" at the age of eleven to the end of his life, Samuel served God faithfully and with absolute obedience to His word. Though he was not king, it was this man who truly led a nation in difficult times.

A Willing and Obedient Heart

It does not take much for God to use a person. Samuel was born to a woman who felt forgotten and empty, but because he was listening for God and had a willing heart, he was chosen to be the voice of the Lord to God's most beloved people. That should give hope to you and me.

If you will adopt a similar heart as Samuel's and be willing to listen, God will indeed speak to you. You might miss the mark the first time or two, just like Samuel when he mistook God's voice for Eli's. Perhaps you will move on something too early or, in spite of good intentions, maybe you will move based on what seems good to you. But if you continue to stay rooted and grounded in the Lord, listening for His voice, He will not allow any failure He cannot redeem.

I know that firsthand. I once came off a mountaintop experience when I heard from God, acted and then made a significant misstep on the very next move. I missed God, and this was on the heels of stepping out in faith and getting it right. But you know what? It all turned out okay.

The point is, listening to the voice of God takes time and practice. You might get it wrong at times, but if you will be open to His voice, I promise you will hear Him. Once you do, there are no limits to how far God will use your willingness.

Imagine what God will do with your "Here I am." There is a hurting world out there, and people all around you looking for hope. When God asks you to step out and lead by example, do not hesitate. Do not hold back your voice. Use it to declare His glory, and watch how your obedience transforms your life and the world around you.

7

ISAIAH, THE PROPHET

The Unconditional "Here I Am"

Life is full of exciting opportunities. It is easy to say, "I'll go," when the task set before us is something enjoyable or does not seem difficult. When it is the dream inside a heart or the promise of a hope fulfilled, we may even jump at the chance to dive in.

Will you help serve in the women's ministry? Yes!

Would you mind leading this Bible study? Of course!

Will you marry me? Heck yeah!

Are you ready to start pushing to deliver that baby? Get him out!

But what if the call is not so easy or will not fulfill an immediate dream? What if the ask will lead you down bumpy roads and dark nights? In these instances we are often not as ready to say yes. It takes more grit, willingness and faith to step out when the call is not lovely.

I came to such a crossroads in my life when I was twenty years old and ready to embark on vocational ministry. I went on a missions trip to the Dominican Republic and fell in love with the people there and the work being done. A few months after my experience, I was offered an internship with the organization and excitedly jumped at the opportunity to serve in that beautiful country for nine months. I still had a few months until my current commitment was over, so I began preparing myself for His use.

I should mention here that about two years before this time I had received the clear call to vocational ministry. Over those two years I had discovered my gift to write and teach, although I was not quite sure where or how I would pursue those passions. When I received this invitation to serve overseas, I assumed missions was my path.

In that gap between receiving the invitation and embarking on the journey, I was asked by my pastor's wife if I would be interested in interning with the children's department for the summer. I greatly respected this woman and felt a prompting in my spirit to pray about it, so I did, even though children's ministry did not exactly get me as excited as foreign missions. I had grown up with three younger brothers and spent most of the prior eight years babysitting them while my parents ran a business, so being surrounded by a bunch of kids did not exactly light a fire in me. Imagine my surprise when I was pretty sure I heard from God that He wanted me to forgo the missions internship and serve in the children's ministry at my church.

Suffice it to say, this was not the easiest yes to make, but looking back, now I can see exactly what God was doing. That internship turned into a career at the church and allowed me to discover my true calling of using the gifts within me to build the local church and minister to women. That simple yes to do something I was not initially excited about forever changed the trajectory of my life, and I am incredibly grateful God guided me along the way. As a bonus, I loved my time with those kiddos and had the opportunity to intentionally pour into a small group of children I still know today—as they embark on careers and make me feel much older.

Life will always present us with opportunities. Sometimes those open doors will lead to a mountaintop, and sometimes they will lead you through a valley. You may go in a direction you never imagined you would take. The question you must ask yourself is, Are you willing to walk through both if God asks you to? Are you willing to say yes to God's call to a difficult journey just as easily as an exciting one?

Isaiah, the prophet, was a man who could say yes to both. Without even knowing what lay ahead, he made himself available to God's plan time and again. But before we jump into his "Here I am" moment, let's take a look at the man himself.

The Evangelical Prophet

Isaiah is often referred to as the evangelical prophet because of his declaration of salvation. In fact, he used the word *salvation* 26 times in the book of Isaiah. By contrast, all the other prophets only used it seven times—combined. He is also quoted in the New Testament more than any other Old Testament prophet, perhaps because he focused heavily on the coming Christ.

What little we know about Isaiah starts with his location, Judah. By the time he was born, Israel had already split into two nations: Israel to the north and Judah to the south. Isaiah lived in Judah and is thought to have been born into a prestigious family, since he had access to the king. He had a wife and two sons and lived in Jerusalem. When God called Isaiah to be His prophet, King Uzziah was reigning.

Isaiah served as a prophet during the reign of four kings: Uzziah, Jotham, Ahaz and Hezekiah. All but Ahaz were considered relatively good kings. Yet, during this time in Judah's history, God's people walked in idolatry. They had abandoned their God.

While Isaiah often prophesied judgment for the nation, God pointed to grace and salvation through him more than any other prophet. I admire the fact that in the midst of harsh messages to the people of Israel, Christ was still revealed in beautiful ways. Through Isaiah, hope was magnified in the hopeless.

Isaiah's "Here I Am"

We find Isaiah's "Here I am" moment in Isaiah 6. But before we get there, let's take a look at what was happening before this moment. Isaiah spends the first five chapters in the book of Isaiah pronouncing a series of judgments against the nation of Judah for their wickedness. He explains how they had forsaken the God who had made them and cared for them, and he goes as far as listing their social sins and describing their abandonment of the Lord. It is a sad declaration of Judah's unfaithfulness. As a natural reaping of what they sowed, judgment was coming, Isaiah declares. However, along with judgment would come the Messiah. Hope was on the horizon.

Isaiah's great "Here I am" moment happened in the early days of Isaiah's ministry, during the year King Uzziah died. Isaiah 6:1–5 tells us:

> In the year that King Uzziah died I saw the LORD sitting upon a throne, high and lifted up; and the train of his robe filled the temple. Above him stood the seraphim. Each had six wings: with two he covered his face, and with two he covered his feet, and with two he flew. And one called to another and said: "Holy, holy, holy is the LORD of hosts; the whole earth is full of his glory!" And the foundations of the thresholds shook at the voice of him who called, and the house was filled with smoke. And I said: "Woe is me! For I am lost; for I am a man of unclean lips, and I dwell in the midst of a people of unclean lips; for my eyes have seen the King, the LORD of hosts!"

At the beginning of Isaiah's vision, great praise is being raised to the Lord Almighty! And who gets to be there witnessing the magnificence? None other than Isaiah. If I had been him, I would have been in awe—and praying they would not realize I was accidentally there and then kick me out. But it was not an accident Isaiah was there; he was a guest invited to a spectacular moment before the throne in heaven.

Instead of pride, Isaiah's first thought was to say that he should not be there beholding God's glory. As I read this passage, I am always reminded of the grace of God, not only toward Isaiah but toward me, toward us, even today. It is so relatable to me that Isaiah's first thought was "Woe is me! For I am lost; for I am a man of unclean lips." He knew he was but a sinful man. How should he be before the Lord of Hosts? Who was he to be part of something so spectacular? In the same vein, who are any of us—who are you and I—that we should know God?

While Isaiah felt unworthy to be in the presence of holiness, God affirmed that he was right where He wanted him to be and made a way for him to remain in His presence. After Isaiah realized and proclaimed his sin, the seraphim touched his lips with a burning coal from the altar of incense.

> Then one of the seraphim flew to me, having in his hand a burning coal that he had taken with tongs from the altar. And he touched my mouth and said: "Behold, this has touched your lips; your guilt is taken away, and your sin atoned for."
>
> Isaiah 6:6–7

Through this symbolic encounter with the angel and the burning coal, Isaiah was extended atonement and grace before the throne.

His vision is a portrait of the atonement extended to us in our own sinfulness. Purging sin hurts and is never easy, and repentance is painful. But although the fires of purification burn, they are necessary. Once our uncleanliness has been taken away, then we are sanctified and made ready for service.

Can we just pause a moment and personalize this incredible moment? Place yourself in Isaiah's shoes, because this is a picture of our access to God and how He makes it possible for us to enter into His presence. Do we deserve to be welcomed there? Nope. Do we deserve to be invited into His plan? Surely not. Do we deserve to be atoned for? Heck no. But you serve a good and gracious Father who longs to connect with you, use you and who will orchestrate all the details of your life like a fine symphony to bring reconciliation and divine purpose. He sent His only Son to make atonement for your sins so that one day you could stand before His throne and cry with the angels, "Holy, holy, holy!"

Only after Isaiah's lips were touched and he was made clean did he receive his commission. Verse 8 says Isaiah "heard the voice of the LORD saying, 'Whom shall I send, and who will go for us?'" This is the only "Here I am" moment in which God did not call a specific name. He was simply asking who was available. He was looking for someone willing to go. Not surprisingly, Isaiah's response was immediate: "Here I am! Send me" (v. 8).

When Isaiah heard God ask for someone to send, he did not hesitate to volunteer. Honestly, he did not even know what he was signing up for. He had no idea what God was planning. But it did not matter. God had sanctified him, and he was ready and eager to serve God; it did not matter what the task was.

Using Your Voice

Isaiah was not perfect, nor was he necessarily the most qualified messenger. He was simply sanctified and willing. That is it. That is all God is looking for in the people He uses.

Let's take a look at both of those factors that qualified Isaiah— that qualify us—for service to God. As you read, evaluate how you align with those qualities.

Sanctification

John MacArthur said this about Isaiah's call in chapter 6:

God isn't looking for great, intellectual brilliance. He isn't looking for oratorical skill. He isn't looking for literary genius. He's not looking for the movers and the shakers and the power brokers, and He's not looking for those people that the world assumes to be the leaders of choice. What He's looking for is people who have been cleansed.[1]

God is not looking for the most eloquent or charismatic person to go forth and make a difference in this world; He is looking for sanctification, for those who have brought their sin to Him and been covered in the blood of Christ. When Isaiah stood there in the presence of holiness, he was keenly aware of his sin. There was no brushing it under the rug or putting on a good show. He did not run away from God in shame and allow it to keep him in bondage, like so many of us do. He saw his sin and his need for sanctification, and he was honest about it. Isaiah laid it all out there at the foot of the throne. And because he was willing to deal with it, he was cleansed and made righteous. That was one of only two things that qualified him for the ministry God was calling him to.

If you long to start walking out the plans and purposes God has for your life but feel stuck, unable to live out your calling, a wise first step is to evaluate the state of your heart. Let's get really personal here for just a moment and talk as friends. If I were sitting down with you right now over coffee I would ask, "Friend, how is your heart?" In other words, where are you struggling? What is God asking you to lay down? What sin is lingering in the shadows because you have not confessed it yet? I truly believe these are the questions God is wanting you to ask yourself right now, not to make you feel condemned or guilty but so He can cleanse you from all unrighteousness. God sent His only Son to take your sin upon Himself and take the punishment so that you do not have to. Will you receive this beautiful gift? Will you embrace His sanctification of your heart, soul and spirit? When you have embraced this vulnerability, acknowledged your unrighteousness and confessed your sin, God will forgive you. He will make you white as snow.

Willingness

The other characteristic we see Isaiah display in chapter 6 is willingness. Isaiah was a man who simply made himself available for what God was doing. He did not bring a game plan to God, nor did he hide from Him. Isaiah just said, "Here I am!" and God used those three words to use Isaiah to speak to a nation.

Roger and Joy's story portrays this same willingness so well. It always gives me goosebumps.

A few years back, Roger, Joy and their children were living fairly comfortable lives in Missouri when God interrupted their routine. Roger had a steady job, and although he was feeling a stirring in his heart God might have other plans in the future, he did not have any specific leading about next steps. Joy was at home with their kids, and they were heavily involved in their church. They had family around, and as far as they were concerned, they would always be where they were.

As time went on, Roger could not shake the feeling that God was stirring him to do something different. He began interviewing for jobs he was very qualified for in an attempt to discern if God wanted him to make a change, but after nine months of dead-end interviews and many near misses, Roger had not received a single offer. During this job search, their church rallied together for a Daniel fast, and the couple had three prayer requests: clarity for Roger's job, to be used by God and for their borders of influence to expand. Not long after the fast, a job opportunity presented itself to Roger—an opportunity that seemed too good to be true. It seemed to be an answer to their prayers.

The next Sunday, however, Roger and Joy received a prophetic word from a woman in their congregation. She said God was leading her to tell them to stop and turn around. They began to pray if this job opportunity was from the Lord, and sure enough, that week the offer fell apart.

After this disappointment, they questioned if they were really hearing from God. In answer to their prayer, all the work God was doing behind the scenes began to take shape before their eyes. First, Joy was reading in Joshua, and the words came alive. She felt prompted in her heart to share with Roger that he was to halt his job search. Together they believed that God had something worked out already, and they renewed their commitment to be faithful with where they were and with what they had.

Then, nearly a month later, Roger prayed a specific prayer: *God, give me clarity this weekend regarding Your plan.* Two days later his prayer was answered. That Sunday was Vision Sunday at their church, a time when the church looked back and celebrated all God had done the previous year and also cast a vision for the new year. In his explanation of what was coming for their church family, the pastor laid out their plan to launch a new campus in Joplin, roughly two hours away. Joy's heart began to pound, and she felt God was speaking to her spirit that this was what He had for them.

When the family got in the car after service, Joy wanted to share what was on her heart but waited to see if Roger brought it up. Sure enough, before they had even left the parking lot, Roger asked what Joy thought about Joplin. That night, the two talked, and both firmly believed God was calling them to uproot and leave everything they knew to go to a new city and minister to that community as volunteers at the new campus.

The pieces they had prayed about for a year began falling into place. Roger was quickly offered two incredible jobs in Joplin. The one he accepted was better than anything he had applied for back home the year prior. Not only was it a great job working for a Christian owner, but the salary was significantly better than anything available to him in his industry before then. Today, the family is living in Joplin and part of a vibrant, growing church.

When Roger and Joy stepped out in obedience, they had no idea what God had in store. Regardless, they trusted Him and His plan for their lives and had a willingness to be used. In response, God blessed them and has been able to bless a whole community through them. He will do the same for you, if you will only trust Him.

Are you willing and available to God, whatever the call may be? If God comes to you looking for someone to use—whether to walk out your dream or to do something you had never thought you would do—will you throw your hand up in the air with enthusiasm and say, "Me," like Roger, Joy and Isaiah?

Further, are you ready to move when God calls? God wants to use you to reach people who are hurting, who are broken and lost and who are suffering and know no way out. God is asking you, friend, in this very moment, "Will you go for Me now? Are you ready to step outside of everything you know or thought you knew and tell people about Me and about how I transformed your life? Will you tell them I want to do the same for them?"

If so, your "Here I am" of willingness to God—of being available for Him to use, whatever the call—will be a conduit He uses to speak truth and hope to unbelieving people. Who knows how that will change the world.

8

ANANIAS, THE DISCIPLE

The "Here I Am" That Overcomes Fear

Ananias is where this journey all started for me. I was sitting curled up on my couch with a cup of hot coffee reading Acts 9 when I read that a man I knew little about responded to God with a powerful phrase. My curiosity was piqued, because I felt as if I had heard this phrase before. I pulled out some of my study resources and came across the various "Here I am" statements we explore now. I was immediately drawn to the value of these three words, and thus began a two-year journey of study and prayer.

Acts 9 focuses primarily on the conversion of Saul, whom God would use in tremendous ways. We all know him as Paul and find him woven so prominently throughout the New Testament Scriptures. Because of the tall shadow Paul casts and the significance of his conversion experience, it may be easy to overlook the supporting role of Ananias in that story, but Ananias is nonetheless a man of great value in our own faith journey.

We do not know much about Ananias because he is referenced only twice in Scripture. From Acts 9 we gather that he was a disciple of Jesus who lived in Damascus. In Acts 22, Paul says Ananias was well spoken of by the Jews and gives a brief account of Ananias' role in Paul's conversion. That is it. Those two places provide all the information we have.

To clear up any misidentification, I want to address that this is not the same Ananias found in Acts 5 who, with his wife Sapphira, sold his property and kept a portion of the proceeds for himself. Nor is this Ananias the high priest in Acts 23–24 who brought a case against Paul. Our Ananias was a regular guy who loved Jesus, just like you and me.

The Backstory on Saul

To fully understand the significance of Ananias' "Here I am" statement, it is crucial that we first study the character of Saul. Saul was born in Tarsus, a very large trade center in the Mediterranean that was in the Roman province of Cilicia. He was born to a wealthy Jewish family, his father both a Roman citizen and a Pharisee from the tribe of Benjamin. His education was top notch, and history tells us Saul even sat under the teaching of one of the leading rabbis of the first century. Saul really had everything going for him.

Saul himself was a noted Pharisee of his time—a rising star, you might say—known throughout the Jewish world for persecuting those who followed Jesus Christ. In fact, the first reference to him in the Bible is in Acts 7 at the stoning of Stephen. Verse 58 recounts, "Then they cast him [Stephen] out of the city and stoned him. And the witnesses laid down their garments at the feet of a young man named Saul." By the description given in this verse, we gather that Saul was heavily involved in the act. Furthermore, Acts 8:1 says that "Saul approved of his execution."

After the death of Stephen, things were not very pretty for the early Church, and much of that had to do with Saul. Beginning in Jerusalem, he led a great persecution of anyone who believed in Jesus Christ as Savior. Acts 8:3 says, "But Saul was ravaging the church, and entering house after house, he dragged off men and women and committed them to prison." Many of the believers in Jerusalem scattered to outlying regions for safety.

Saul's zeal for persecuting Christians only grew with time, as did the reach of his hatred.

> But Saul, still breathing threats and murder against the disciples of the Lord, went to the high priest and asked him for letters to the synagogues at Damascus, so that if he found any belonging to the Way, men or women, he might bring them bound to Jerusalem.
>
> Acts 9:1–2

Saul was not satisfied with executing the believers in Jerusalem; he wanted to take it further. Saul aimed to head to Damascus, the capital city of Syria, which was 160 miles north of Jerusalem. He was approaching that city with his servants when a bright light shone, and he fell to the ground. A loud voice permeated the scene, asking Saul why he was persecuting Christians. "Falling to the ground," Saul inquired, "Who are you?" (vv. 4–5). The voice replied, "I am Jesus, whom you are persecuting" (v. 5). The Lord then told him to go into the city and await instructions.

As if the shock of his life-changing encounter with Christ was not disorienting enough, Saul also lost his sight. For three days Saul sat in Damascus, blind and unsure of what awaited him.

Ananias' "Here I Am"

Ananias enters the story at this point and gets his "Here I am" moment right away. Acts 9:10 tells us "there was a disciple at

Damascus named Ananias. The Lord said to him in a vision, 'Ananias.' And he said, 'Here I am, Lord.'"

I love that Ananias knew it was the Lord talking. He knew exactly what the Lord's voice sounded like, and he had the ear to recognize it. That in and of itself is so encouraging to me. I want to be a person who has developed such sensitivity to the voice of God that I am able to hear His voice above the whispers of the world. To be that dialed in, Ananias had to have spent many hours in prayer, study and obedience. Little did he know that obedience was about to be put to the test.

God proceeded to tell Ananias that He wanted him to go to a specific house in Damascus to meet "a man of Tarsus named Saul" (v. 11). It is not surprising that when God told Ananias to go to Saul, he was surprised—and likely fearful. Ananias was not clueless. He knew who Saul was. Ananias had heard all of the awful things Saul had done to the believers, and he had already heard that Saul was coming to Damascus to arrest believers. In fact, he probably felt walking right up to Saul would surely bring trouble upon him and perhaps even lead to death.

There is often fear when God calls us to do something. It is important to note that Ananias did not run away or avoid Saul, as many may have done, knowing Saul's reputation. Instead, he left right away to find Saul. Yes, he may have felt the fear common to us all; however, he responded promptly, which is uncommon.

We can connect with Ananias' concerns, right? We can understand the fear associated with taking a big risk: leaving a secure job for one across the country or perhaps taking a step of faith so big there is no job at all; losing someone and finding a way to move on and establish a new normal; confronting a harsh past and embracing a new future; or driving across the country to the Wyoming wilderness. Whatever the catalyst, fear hits us all at various times and in various ways.

One Decision. Huge Impact.

I cannot help but chuckle a bit. I wonder how much faster Ananias might have walked on his way to find Saul if only he had known what was about to happen. I do not think he could have imagined in his wildest dreams what God was about to unleash through Saul. It is a bit of a hint for us that as we conquer our fears to pursue the call of God, He will do more than we could ever imagine.

Ananias indeed found Saul and laid his hands on him, and Saul regained his sight. Immediately, Ananias prophesied over him and baptized him. He had the incredible opportunity to witness the transformation of a persecutor into a mighty man of God. Knowing Saul's reputation, I can imagine that Ananias must have felt some sense of how big this moment was. If Saul had been zealous for the persecution of believers, surely he would be zealous for the Lord!

To get the full scope of how significant Paul's conversion was, it is beneficial to look at the impact of his ministry. Right after his encounter with Ananias, Paul's zeal for the Lord led him to witness. The first thing he did when he got saved was go to the synagogue and proclaim Jesus as the Son of God. Can you imagine what the synagogue leaders and believers in the city were thinking? They expected the great Pharisee Saul to show up and start arresting people who proclaimed Jesus. Instead, he showed up and started proclaiming Jesus himself! It is amazing how God can take the worst among sinners, as Paul would call himself (1 Timothy 1:15), and make a mighty warrior in the kingdom of God.

What happened to Paul after his bold preaching in the Damascus synagogue? Galatians 1 recounts that for the next three years he spent time in Arabia and Damascus, where he was taught by the Lord personally. From there it was a long road. He went on three missionary journeys, healing people and witnessing through the power of the Holy Spirit. He penned fourteen letters that would later become books in the New Testament. While he faced many trials for Christ, God used him to do great things that expanded the early Church.

The ripple effect of Paul's and Ananias' faithful trust and obedience still echoes on today. All those transformations accredited to Paul will also be credited to Ananias at the judgment seat of Christ, when Christians are rewarded for what they did on earth.

What fear, if any, inserts doubts? Pokes at your desire to walk in obedience? Holds you back from forward movement? Let Ananias' story inspire you to face your fears for the glory of God and the transformation of others. Your "Here I am" will leave a powerful ripple effect in the Kingdom of God, even if you do not see it this side of heaven.

9

OLD TESTAMENT PILLARS

The Bible is full of men and women whose lives were marked by faith and obedience, even though they may not have uttered the phrase, "Here I am." Their stories are full of awe, and they too exemplified the kind of courage that is building up like a fire in our souls from studying these testimonies. As we see how God used them for extraordinary feats, my prayer is that you will see yourself in their experiences and know like never before that through God anything is possible.

I encourage you not to just breeze through these examples but to take your time gleaning from their stories. If one or two hit close to home, go to the Word and dive deeper into their lives, and ask God how you can grow in carrying a "Here I am" spirit.

Israel's Faithful

The Old Testament is full of wonderful, normal people God used to do amazing things. It is why I love the Old Testament so much. It is such an encouragement to see people like me mess up, find redemption and be used by God. It makes me feel a little less crazy and bolsters my faith.

Joseph

Joseph has been immortalized in contemporary culture through Broadway's *Joseph and the Amazing Technicolor Dreamcoat* and Disney's *Prince of Egypt*. His incredible story of triumph and the reach of a dream is inspiring. The guy left quite the mark on this world, and there is a reason for that. His trust in the Lord is to be admired. Joseph is also an obvious contender for a "Here I am" honorary mention, as he was someone who authentically walked out a willingness to serve God, no matter what.

Joseph was born to Jacob, whom we met earlier in the book. He was the long-prayed-for son of Rachel, and he was dearly loved by his parents. In truth, he was a favorite of Jacob's, and his brothers knew it. It did not help that Joseph had prophetic dreams that showed his brothers bowing before him—dreams Joseph told his brothers all about. This meant family drama yet again for Jacob's clan.

One day Joseph's brothers, who were totally fed up with him, saw a chance to get rid of him. They sold him into slavery. Yep, you read that right. Slavery. He was taken to Egypt, where he was then sold again to a man of prominence named Potiphar.

I cannot imagine the loneliness and trauma that Joseph experienced during this time. He must have felt as far away from his dreams as possible. After all, how could a slave ever rise to influence? If I were Joseph, I would have been pretty darn discouraged at that point, yet he never gave up.

Joseph worked hard and honorably. God's favor was on him, and everything Joseph touched was blessed. Because of this favor and through his obedience, Potiphar appointed him head of his household and entrusted everything to him. The Bible says Potiphar did not concern himself with anything except what to eat because he trusted Joseph completely to oversee all that he had. What a testament to being faithful with what we are given. It so inspires me to do my creative best with what has been given to me.

After a while Potiphar's wife attempted to entice Joseph to sleep with her. When he did not, she claimed he tried to rape her. This lie landed Joseph in prison. Even though he did not give up while in slavery, this situation would have served up a pretty good reason for Joseph to throw in the towel.

But again, Joseph did not waver. And as a result of his faithfulness, God showed him favor through the warden, who entrusted the care of the prisoners to Joseph. Once again, Joseph rose to a place of leadership, all of which was preparing him for a promotion that seemed impossible.

Eventually Joseph was given the opportunity to interpret a dream the pharaoh had. Though none of the pharaoh's soothsayers could interpret it, Joseph rightly discerned that his dream essentially warned of a coming famine. Recognizing Joseph's value, the pharaoh appointed Joseph as second-in-command over Egypt. The impossible was made possible! What's more, while serving in that role, Joseph's dream from his youth came true: His brothers traveled to Egypt, bowed before him and asked him for help.

Although his incredible rise from slavery to second-in-command was ultimately all due to God and His favor, Joseph's obedience and faithfulness made it possible for him to receive those blessings from the Lord. His willingness to be diligent with the little God entrusted to him placed him in a position to be blessed and used by God.

What I appreciate most about Joseph is his childlike faith. The guy was so expectant of what God was going to do, even in dire situations. He was enthusiastic about his God-given dreams, even though it caused family drama. Because of his faith, he remained an all-around good guy in the ups and downs of his roller-coaster-ride life.

Joseph's story is an encouragement for anyone struggling to find the endurance to be faithful when things get hard. Perhaps it seems no matter what you do, everything just falls apart. Maybe you wonder, What is the point? Why give your best to what seems fruitless? Friend, I hear you. In fact, I feel the burden of those questions. I have been there! In a season of tedious routine and on the heels of disappointment, I have wondered the same thing. I have struggled to keep going. But this story is such a strong testament to the fruit that obedience and faithfulness bear. If God could order Joseph's steps, even when the situation looked bleak, He will guide our journey as well.

Instead of playing these questions of doubt over and over again in your head, get in the Word and read God's promises. Start with this story in Genesis 37–47 and tell yourself that God honors the faithful. He does! Then, one step at a time, be obedient. Give your best to the small things entrusted to you, and watch your faithfulness bear fruit. Furthermore, watch God entrust you with more.

David

David is perhaps one of the most famous people in the Bible, and you likely already know a thing or two about him. You probably know that he was a man after God's own heart, as the Bible says, and that he also made some mistakes along the way. Yet through it all God worked all things for good and used David in tremendous, destiny-altering ways.

David exemplified living life with a "Here I am" attitude toward the Lord. Over and over again he showed he was willing to do whatever God asked of him. *Take on Goliath.* "Okay." *Be the king of Israel.* "Yes, Lord." *But wait many years to assume the throne, and in the meantime, run for your life while Saul tries to kill you.* "Sure." *Put together all the plans to build a temple for Me, but then pass it on to your son to accomplish.* "Okay." There are so many instances when God said to go, and David went right away. But there are also instances when God said, "Wait," or, "Not yet," and David waited. Whatever God wanted from David, David was on board.

Yes, he made mistakes along the way, but David always came to the throne of grace in true repentance. Overall, he chose to follow and honor God, no matter what the gain or cost.

Are you willing to do the same? Are you willing to go when God says to go and wait when God says to wait? Your flesh may fight such obedience, but to say, "Here I am," is to live a life in accordance with God's desires. When you get intimately close to Him, as David did, His desires become yours. It becomes your natural heartbeat to ebb and flow with the Father when you are divinely connected to Him through a "Here I am" faith.

Noble Women

Women have always been a part of God's redemptive and restorative plan for mankind. He has used His daughters in powerful and bold ways to lead, set people free, take the first step of faith and so much more. Women are His heartbeat and His hands on earth for Kingdom purposes.

The Old Testament tells the stories of some powerhouse women and how their "Here I am" hearts left big imprints in the Bible and on history.

Rahab

Rahab was not the wife of some noble man, nor was she a woman of power. Instead, she was a prostitute, a woman considered by many to be disgraced and unworthy. Her past did not qualify her for God's big plans, but her sensitive heart made her a prime candidate for redemption. Because of her humility, Rahab made it possible for Israel to take Jericho.

We meet her right before the battle of Jericho. Joshua had sent two spies into Jericho in order that they might take the city and claim their Promised Land, but the king found out they were there and tried to find and kill them. Rahab took the spies in and protected them from the king and his soldiers. She had heard about the God of the Israelites, and she believed He was true and powerful enough to give Israel the victory over Jericho. Because of her faith, she extended safety to the spies, and when Jericho was taken, she and her family were spared.

Rahab made a seemingly small decision to grant safety to two men, but because of that choice her life was spared. More than that, she was grafted into the family of God. She would become the mother of Boaz, a godly man who is included in the genealogy of Jesus.

Here's the honest truth: None of us are worthy of the incredible plans God has in store for us. I certainly do not feel worthy to be used by God to share these words. My past is a mess! But God is not looking for the people who got it right the most or who are the most qualified by the world's terms. Instead, God is looking for those who are available. He is looking for the humble and for those who will say, "I believe in You," and then step forward in His plan. Do you fit that description?

Your past is not an indicator of your future. Rahab would not have measured up to man's idea of the word *qualified*, but in God's eyes, she was found available and worthy of salvation. God looks at the heart, and that is all that matters to Him. If you have a heart that says "Here I am" to God and a willingness to step out in faith and obedience, He will use you in amazing ways.

Ruth

We see God moving throughout the entire book of Ruth. His fingerprints are all over her life. Like Rahab, Ruth was not born into the family of God. She was an outsider who encountered God in the midst of her pain and chose to follow Him. As a result, she too was grafted into His family. In fact, Ruth was grafted into Rahab's family tree through Rahab's son Boaz, whom she married. But Ruth's story started long before she met Boaz.

The book of Ruth tells us that there was a family living in Israel—a man, woman and their two sons—who picked up and moved to the neighboring country of Moab to escape the famine in Israel. Though Moab had been spared from the famine, it was a nation that did not follow God. While there, the two sons met and married Moabite women, and one of those women was Ruth. Eventually, all the men in the family died, leaving only Ruth, her sister-in-law and her mother-in-law, Naomi.

After her husband and sons died, Naomi chose to return to Bethlehem, where she was from and still had family. Ruth chose to go with her. This was a major decision and step of faith for the Moabite woman, as she would have been unfamiliar with the people and customs in Israel. She would not know anyone but Naomi. Ruth was leaving everything and everyone she knew behind for the unknown.

Ruth is one of my favorite people in the Bible, and I would encourage you to go read her story. As with the others in this chapter, there were no grand "Here I am" moments in her history, but she fits here among the faithful who answered God's call because her journey was made up of one small "Here I am" after another—a trail of little choices she made to follow God and be obedient wherever God led her. She gave no thought to pride or past hurt or to what was comfortable. It was her submission to God that led her to redemption.

Go to Israel, the land of My people. "Here I am."
Take care of your bitter mother-in-law. "Here I am."
Follow the customs of the people. "Here I am."
Pursue My way even though you mourn and hurt. "Here I am."
Go to Boaz, the man who will redeem you and your family, and marry him. "Here I am."

Ruth's life and legacy teach us that sometimes a "Here I am" is making the right choice, one decision at a time. It determined the trajectory of her life, and it will do the same in yours.

Deborah

In the gap of time after Joshua died and before Saul was made king, God appointed judges in times of crisis to lead Israel under His guidance. We can read about this time in the book of Judges, which tells the stories of people like Gideon and Samson. But there is one judge who stands out, and her name was Deborah. Yes, you read that right. God appointed a woman to serve as judge in a time and culture where women seldom held leadership roles.

Before Deborah was appointed, Israel had once again strayed, and as a result they had been given into the hands of their enemy, the Canaanites. The people called out to God for deliverance, and as a result, God called Deborah to step out and lead.

Initially Deborah was described as a judge over settling disputes, but she was also a prophetess whom God would speak through. In the face of adversity from their enemy, she called for Barak, a military leader at the time, and told him that God wanted to use him to lead their people in victory over the Canaanites. Barak doubted the call, however, and asked Deborah to go with him. Deborah agreed and went to battle with Barak, and victory was given to Israel. Her significant "Here I am" moment was not this divine moment of enlightening but rather a simple step into an area of need.

Sometimes your "Here I am" might mean standing in the gap or filling a vacancy, like Deborah did. The prayer team is low on volunteers, and God is asking you to serve. Perhaps you feel led to facilitate community in your neighborhood and be a light to hurting neighbors. Whatever the situation, if you see a need, step in and serve. As with Isaiah and Deborah, God is looking for those who make themselves available and willing. Where does your life intersect with those needs?

Esther

Esther was a Jew raised in Persia by her cousin Mordecai, and the Bible says that she was beautiful. Through a series of events, she was essentially placed in a beauty pageant before King Xerxes so that he could choose a wife. Esther was chosen, and she became queen over a land in which her people were foreigners.

Some time later an official named Haman was placed in the highest command under Xerxes, but he was a man of significant pride. When Mordecai did not bow down to him at the city gate one day, Haman devised a plan not only to get rid of Mordecai but to get rid of all the Jews living in Persia. He took his plan to King Xerxes under the guise that the Jews were unruly to the king's laws. At Haman's request, an edict was signed that gave permission for all Jews to be destroyed. Mordecai heard of the edict and pleaded with Esther to reveal her heritage to the king and do what no one else could do: save their people.

This was not as easy as you might think. Esther was not guaranteed access to her husband, nor was she sure the king would hear her out, even if she did get the opportunity to share. Esther went before Xerxes in spite of the unfavorable circumstances, and she was granted access to him. With great humility, she exposed Haman's plan and made her plea for her people. Xerxes was angered at the news and had Haman killed. He also sent out an edict that all Jews could defend themselves. On the day of reckoning, anyone who came against a Jew was destroyed. Instead of a genocide, it was a day of victory for the people.

Esther was called to take up a cause and act, even though it could have meant death for her. She stepped up to the plate under these words made famous by Mordecai: "Who knows whether you have not come to the kingdom for such a time as this?" (Esther 4:14).

Who knows why you are here, right now? Perhaps only God. But if He has called you here and now for such a task, it must be for a reason. He wants to use you and is inviting you into His good, beautiful plan of redemption for all. Will you step up to the plate like Esther did, or will you hide in fear?

The Captives

Daniel, Shadrach, Meshach and Abednego lived and served God in captivity before Esther's story. Like her, they were Israelite by heritage but Babylonian by citizenship. They were people far from home and living life in a pagan culture away from the norms of their Jewish heritage. Each was a brave and courageous advocate for God Almighty in the face of oppression and persecution. Their faith and obedience among foreign people and ungodly influences stand out magnificently in a bleak time in Israel's history.

Daniel

Oh, Daniel. How faithful he was—so faithful, in fact, that twice in Daniel 6 he is noted as someone who "continually" served God (vv. 16 and 20). Few people in the Bible are as unwavering as he was, which is quite impressive considering he spent most of his life living in a pagan culture and was often tempted to give in to idolatry.

Daniel was a teenager of Jewish nobility when Babylon seized Jerusalem. Because he was deemed skillful and competent—a valuable new asset to the king—Daniel was taken captive and brought to Babylon to serve in King Nebuchadnezzar's court. There he made a name for himself as a man of honor and wisdom, and as one who could interpret dreams.

From the beginning of his time in the palace, he pursued righteousness in the midst of temptation and was rewarded for it over and over again. While still new to the court, he was offered fine food and wine but refused such delicacies because he did not want to defile himself. As a result, he was given favor in the palace, and that favor extended until his death. Even when Babylon was captured by Persia, Daniel continued to find favor with the sitting king and was placed in a prominent position time and again.

Not everyone was so enamored with him, however. When a new king named Darius took the throne in Daniel's later years and set Daniel over the whole kingdom, this did not sit well with the other officials. They began to brew a plot to discredit Daniel and destroy his reputation with the king. When they could not find any fault with him, they petitioned the king to sign an injunction making it illegal to pray to anyone but Darius for thirty days. Darius did not know what this would do to his favorite official, but the officials knew Daniel was faithful to his God and that this would mean eventual judgment for their rival.

Even in the face of opposition, Daniel remained steadfast. I love that the Bible shows us that as soon as Daniel heard about the signed document, he went straight to his house and praised God. He continued doing this multiple times a day every day, as he had been.

When it was brought to Darius' attention that Daniel had broken the law, he tried everything possible to save Daniel. In fact, Daniel 6:14 tells us that "he labored till the sun went down to rescue him." But the other officials petitioned for Darius to follow through on his injunction, and as a result Daniel was thrown into the lions' den.

We would be missing a huge part of the story if we neglected to explore Darius' response to these events. First, he tried to find a way to save Daniel, his most trusted official. When that did not work, he did something very unusual for someone of his position and background. The entire night Daniel was in the den, Darius did not sleep but instead fasted. The pagan king fasted! As soon as the sun rose the next morning, he rushed to the den to check on Daniel. His prayers had been answered. He found Daniel alive!

In Beth Moore's phenomenal study *Daniel: Lives of Integrity, Words of Prophecy* she points out that one of the highlights of his story is the way we "see a worldly Darius become impressed with our God."[1] Daniel's decision to say "Here I am" to God in spite of the threat of death changed the king. After God delivered Daniel from the lions' den, Darius chose to serve Him. A pagan king from a far-off nation chose to worship God Almighty because of one man's obedience. Darius was so impacted by the experience that he then issued a decree for the whole nation to worship God alone. A whole nation was pointed to God! Truth be told, Daniel's decisions to remain faithful in the face of adversity always affected the unbelievers around him; Darius was not the only one moved by Daniel's unwavering obedience.

Every day you have a choice either to be faithful no matter what may come or to crack under the weight of temptation. Daniel's life shows you and me that when we choose righteousness over sin, it will change our lives and others'. Saying "Here I am" to obedience when things are not easy can facilitate the opportunity for an unbeliever to be pointed to God. And what's more, that "wordly Darius" reached by your example could be someone who goes on to have major influence or impact for God's Kingdom down the road. You might not be in the king's court, but the teenager in your church you make time to pour into might one day preach the Gospel to millions. Your commitment to integrity at work could influence your CEO and change the trajectory of his journey and a whole company.

When I think of people in my life whose faithful example has borne fruit in others' lives, I think of a man by the name of Dick Foth. Dick was born in California in the first half of the last century, as he cleverly put it when I interviewed him. A pastor's kid, Dick spent his formative years in between California, India and Missouri. He gave his heart to Jesus at seven years old and in high school felt a tug into vocational ministry.

There was just one thing holding him back: a stutter. From the ages of 8 to 25 years old, he had one, and it was this characteristic that held him back from going to Bible school. Dick could not imagine anyone would want to hear a preacher stutter, so he began premed studies at Cal Berkeley. But it was while he was in college, as he was reading the Sermon on the Mount, that he knew he could not fight this call on his life anymore. Dick transferred to Bethany Bible College and later got his master's at Wheaton College in Illinois.

After graduation, Dick had a desire to pursue missions in India but was required to complete two years as a senior pastor first. Those two years turned into an unexpected twelve years at a church. Afterward, he was offered the role of president at his alma mater, Bethany Bible College. At 36, Dick assumed that position.

Being a college president wore Dick out. After fourteen years he was tired and burnt out. This midlife break led to a year of traveling the country doing ministry here and there. Then an opportunity arose, one that did not really make sense at first. In his fifties, Dick and his wife were offered the chance to work with a ministry in Washington, D.C. There was no office—or starting pay—but Dick knew God was in it, so they moved across the country with a "Here I am" heart.

When Dick shared his story with me, he talked about how he was great at going wide with many but not deep with a few. He also said there were two types of people he felt awkward around as a minister: the wealthy and those who were specialists in their areas. As it turned out, God's call required him to overcome that weakness and his fear of engaging those two groups.

For the next fifteen years, Dick simply built relationships with the influencers of our nation. There was no agenda except genuine friendship. Interestingly enough, he ended up embracing the very things that once made him nervous. He was surrounded by the wealthy and influential and those who were specialists in their fields, and he focused on going deep with these few.

Dick ended up spending a significant amount of time in the offices and homes of senators, ranking military officials and the attorney general at the time. While everybody was out to leverage relationship for gain, Dick offered a trustworthy friendship with no strings attached. It was this commitment to love others that allowed him the opportunity to influence influencers.

His "Here I am" opened the door wide for him to pray with, break bread and have meaningful conversations with some of the country's most powerful people.

Daniel's and Dick's stories show us we are never too ordinary to do extraordinary things for the Kingdom. If God could use the faithfulness of Daniel, who was taken captive as a teenager in a foreign land, to influence a king and country, He can use you. If God could turn Dick's areas of weakness into strengths, He can do the same in your life. Your determination to pursue God in the face of adversity and struggle will have a ripple effect you may only truly see once you reach eternity.

Shadrach, Meshach and Abednego

Shadrach, Meshach and Abednego were good friends with Daniel. In fact, like him, these three men were youths of nobility in Jerusalem who were carried off to Babylon. They too refused to eat from the king's offerings and were given favor with the kings of the land because of their faithfulness and obedience to God.

You have likely heard their story of the fiery furnace. Years before Daniel was thrown in the lions' den, King Nebuchadnezzar built a giant golden statue and placed it before the nation. The king gathered his officials, which included Shadrach, Meshach and Abednego, for the dedication and gave the decree that when a noise sounded, all should fall down and worship the idol. When the noise came, the three men refused to worship—and were brought forth for punishment for neglecting to do so.

Next to the idol, the king had set up a fiery furnace for anyone who refused to obey his command. When Shadrach, Meshach and Abednego did not worship the idol, they were brought before the king and commanded once more to obey. Here is how they responded:

King Nebuchadnezzar, we do not need to defend ourselves before you in this matter. If we are thrown into the blazing furnace, the God we serve is able to deliver us from it, and he will deliver us from Your Majesty's hand. But even if he does not, we want you to know, Your Majesty, that we will not serve your gods or worship the image of gold you have set up.

Daniel 3:16–18 NIV

My favorite part is "but even if he does not," because it credits God's goodness, no matter what might happen. These men truly believed that God could protect them from the fire and deliver them from it. But if in His sovereignty He chose not to do that, they still believed God was good. Nothing could make them bow down to a false idol.

As a result of their proclamation they were thrown into the fire, and indeed, God did protect them. What happened next is truly fascinating. The furnace was heated seven times hotter than usual, and the guards who were ordered to throw Shadrach, Meshach and Abednego in were killed by the heat. Yet, the faithful three were not touched. Upon looking into the fire, King Nebuchadnezzar saw four unbound men walking around. The Lord had placed Himself in the fire with His faithful followers and walked the fiery trial with them. How sweet is Jesus! Shadrach, Meshach and Abednego's story is another reminder to us that in our difficulties Jesus is with us.

Nebuchadnezzar beckoned the three men out, and out they came! Not even their hair was singed, nor did they smell of smoke. The fiery furnace had no effect on them because God was with them. As a result, the king gave praise to God and ordered a decree that no one should "say anything against the God of Shadrach, Meshach and Abednego" (Daniel 3:29 NIV). Once again, a nation was changed because three men chose to be obedient to the calling placed on their lives. Their story is yet another reminder that remaining faithful to God in the face of persecution and adversity can echo the goodness of God beyond anything imaginable.

Whatever may stand between you and living out the call of God on your life—none of it is too big for God to overcome. Greater is He who is in you, am I right? I pray you are encouraged by these stories to know that God will take care of the mountains and obstacles before you. He just wants you to say yes. When you do, His provision, coupled with your willing heart, can change the course of history.

10

NEW TESTAMENT LEADERS

The Bible is filled with people who were willing to go when God said go and who stepped out in faith to pursue the unknown, face foes, sacrifice what was dear, step into fiery trials and so much more. And that is all just in the Old Testament! There are still so many powerhouse believers yet to discover in the New Testament. Let's get digging and meet the Christ-followers who carried a "Here I am" heart with them wherever God took them.

Mary and Joseph

Some of the first people we encounter in the New Testament had willing and obedient spirits. They are Mary and Joseph, the parents of Jesus.

Try to remember for just a moment what it was like to be a preteen. Hormones were changing, your body was evolving and emotions were hard to tackle. Now imagine going through such a change while getting engaged and married, talking to angels and becoming the earthly parents of the Son of God. Seems a bit overwhelming, huh? Well, this was Mary and Joseph's reality, or at least Mary's. Many scholars believe she was between twelve and fourteen years old when she became pregnant with Jesus. Knowing this, it is incredible to see the kind of maturity this young girl possessed.

Before we meet her, Mary was an ordinary young girl betrothed to an ordinary man in her village. Then one visit from the angel Gabriel turned her ordinary life upside down.

> In the sixth month the angel Gabriel was sent from God to a city of Galilee named Nazareth, to a virgin betrothed to a man whose name was Joseph, of the house of David. And the virgin's name was Mary. And he came to her and said, "Greetings, O favored one, the Lord is with you!" But she was greatly troubled at the saying, and tried to discern what sort of greeting this might be. And the angel said to her, "Do not be afraid, Mary, for you have found favor with God. And behold, you will conceive in your womb and bear a son, and you shall call his name Jesus. He will be great and will be called the Son of the Most High. And the Lord God will give to him the throne of his father David, and he will reign over the house of Jacob forever, and of his kingdom there will be no end."
>
> Luke 1:26–33

At first, the appearance of the angel shook her a bit. There are few recorded interactions in Scripture between angelic emissaries from God and people anyway, but there had been none for hundreds of years. The God of the universe chose to break His long silence by reaching out to her—this ordinary girl.

Once her fear subsided, Mary must have wondered, *Why me? Who am I?* God was inviting her into the sacred and humbling role of mothering His own Son—a child who would one day lay

146

down His life in order to conquer death and redeem humanity. In spite of her young age, He had seen in her a maturity that was beyond her years and a sensitivity to the things of God. Mary's next step clearly demonstrated why God handpicked her for this honor.

Once Mary had settled a bit, the angel shared more with her.

"The Holy Spirit will come upon you, and the power of the Most High will overshadow you; therefore the child to be born will be called holy—the Son of God. And behold, your relative Elizabeth in her old age has also conceived a son, and this is the sixth month with her who was called barren. For nothing will be impossible with God." And Mary said, "Behold, I am the servant of the Lord; *let it be to me according to your word.*"

Luke 1:35–38, emphasis added

Mary's strong faith and humble heart wasted no time in receiving what God had in store for her. "Let it be to me according to your word" was her "Here I am"; it was her statement of willing, complete and immediate surrender to God. The Scriptures tell us that after that "the angel departed from her" (v. 38), and in the next verse Mary's pregnancy is confirmed in a prophetic encounter with her cousin Elizabeth.

Joseph had a similar experience with an angel of the Lord. When he found out Mary was pregnant before they were married, he planned to break off the engagement discreetly. Then an angel of the Lord appeared to him in a dream. The angel confirmed that Mary had indeed conceived from the Holy Spirit and told him he was to take Mary as his wife. He—Joseph, a carpenter—would raise the One who would save the world from their sins. Like Mary, Joseph obeyed right away.

> When Joseph woke from sleep, he did as the angel of the Lord commanded him: he took his wife, but knew her not until she had given birth to a son. And he called his name Jesus.
>
> Matthew 1:24–25

Mary and Joseph were both ordinary people called to an extraordinary task. Did they hesitate? Not at all! Not in the face of potential judgment from others, an unknown future, doubts about themselves nor their fears. All they knew was that God was calling them to a great journey, and they obeyed. They were faithful. They took on the call and gave it their all.

Has God asked you to do something that came out of left field? Something you were not expecting? Now is not the time to doubt or pull back but instead to walk boldly into the miraculous and wonderful call He has laid out before you. Take the step.

John the Baptist

John the Baptist was the forerunner of Christ. Jesus said about him, "Among those born of women there has risen no one greater than John the Baptist" (Matthew 11:11). It really says something about a person when the Son of God makes such a comment!

John was a relative of Jesus. He was born to Elizabeth, Mary's cousin. Before the two men even entered the world, there was a special bond between them. When their mothers got together while both were pregnant, John actually leapt in Elizabeth's womb, and she was filled with the Holy Spirit and prophesied that Mary would give birth to the Son of God.

John was most known for his ministry baptizing believers on the banks of the Jordan. Thousands heard him preach repentance and were baptized, including Christ. Certainly, Jesus did not have to be baptized by a man, but He did it "to fulfill all righteousness" (Matthew 3:15). It was there on the banks of the muddy river that Jesus' earthly ministry began.

How did John the Baptist show a "Here I am" kind of spirit? He served God faithfully from a young age. He made it his life mission to point people to Christ and always showed humility in the presence of Jesus, even though he had a significant ministry following himself. While other cousins may have experienced some professional rivalry, John never tried to compete with Jesus. Instead, he always pointed people to Christ. He uttered these beautiful words of humility in John 3:30: "He must increase, but I must decrease." It is one of my favorite verses in Scripture and a principle I strive to live by.

When I read about John, I am encouraged to stay the course and to be faithful with all areas of my life. But most importantly, I am reminded to point to Jesus always. If you pick up one thing from John or this chapter or even this book, let it be that Jesus is everything and that the aim of your life should be to point to Him. Always point people to Jesus.

Indeed, one way to do this well is to be a follower who is obedient to the call of God. How might you live your life in order to give your all to this call to point people to Jesus at work, at school, to your friends and family, on social media and more? If this is your desire, pray this prayer with me:

God, I pray now that a fire would be lit in my spirit to be all about You. I pray I would be so committed to You in all areas of my life that there would be a natural outflow that points people to Jesus. Let me decrease so that You can increase in me and so that all others would see is You, my Savior. In Jesus' name, Amen.

Paul

In chapter 8, when we unraveled Ananias' story, we saw that for a long time before his conversion, Paul's "Here I am" was misdirected. He was zealous, yes, but instead of directing that zeal to point people to Jesus, he attempted to turn people away from Him. Once Christ got hold of his life, however, his "Here I am" spirit was used for eternal purposes.

From the moment he put his faith in Jesus, Paul never backed down. He never gave up. He never stopped going to the ends of the earth to tell people about the love of Jesus. For Paul, no ask was too big and no step was too scary to take when God was the one doing the asking. He faced imprisonment, beatings, shipwrecks, persecution and so much more—but none of that stopped him. Paul's heart to be faithful and obedient is unmatched.

The important lesson we learn from Paul's life is that it is never too late to dedicate your life and passion to fulfilling God's plan for you. Paul missed the mark for many years, even though his intentions were good. But when he embraced the sacrifice of Jesus and recalibrated his life to serve God by teaching the risen Christ, there was no slowing him down.

Have you also fumbled in your attempt to do what is right? Maybe you missed the biblical approach to conflict or restoration, and a relationship was lost. Perhaps you had good intentions to pursue an occupation you thought made the most sense, but years later you realize you missed the call of God, and you are starting over in life. Maybe you thought dating that unbeliever seemed like it could work out and that he could eventually come to know Jesus, but now, years later, you are in a hard marriage without a like-hearted teammate. Whatever the specifics, your good intentions failed you, and you hurt others and yourself. From the pages of Paul's story in the Scriptures, God is whispering to your aching soul that there is still hope. You can still follow Him faithfully and make a difference for the Kingdom.

To do so, follow Paul's example. Have your come-to-Jesus moment about how you have tried it on your own and failed. Repent in humility. Spend some serious time with Him.

Now walk forward, deeply connected to the God of new beginnings.

Timothy

Timothy was born to a heathen Greek father and a Jewish mother. Talk about mixed messages! Although he was not circumcised at a young age, likely because of his father, Timothy was taught the Scriptures in his youth. In spite of this somewhat interesting cultural upbringing, he was a normal guy living a pretty normal life in Lystra when Paul came through town on his first missionary journey. When Paul preached the Good News, Timothy was there and quickly committed his life to Christ. He went on to become Paul's beloved son in the faith and a trusted companion of the apostles.

From the moment of his conversion, Timothy was a faithful disciple and often traveled with Paul or served in leadership in the church. He was with Paul on his second and third missionary journeys, taking part in the amazing work God was doing along the way. When not with Paul, he was often stationed where Paul had commissioned him, including serving as the leader of the churches in Asia in Paul's place for a time.

I love when someone in the Bible is relatable, and Timothy is one of those people. He gave his heart to Jesus and faithfully served God wherever he was called. He was obedient and loyal to his spiritual mentor and loved serving in the local church. Timothy was not after notoriety or position; he simply wanted to serve in God's Kingdom, whatever that looked like.

Timothy's life teaches a quiet lesson for those wondering how they might best serve God or who are looking to rise to the top of their field. For Timothy, it was not about how far ahead he could get or how much influence he could garner. And he did not try to have it all figured out. He took obedience one step at a time and was faithful to the call, whatever that looked like. At times that meant leadership, and at times that meant serving under a more prominent Christian figure.

Are you a bit lost in your journey, wondering what is next? If so, remember serving God is not always a miraculous wonder; sometimes it is helping a neighbor or doing some other unseen work. What God cares about is your faithfulness, and a "Here I am" spirit acknowledges this each and every day. It is loyalty and commitment to the cause of Christ that shine through in even the most mundane moments.

Take a cue from Timothy and be faithful with what you have now. Ask yourself, How can you serve God and love others where you are? How can you do your creative best with what is in your hands now? How might you lift up the arms of a leader around you?

If, on the other hand, you are someone desiring to rise to the top and questioning how to get to a greater place of authority, then it is time for surrender. It is time to search your heart and then lay aside the selfish ambitions and get-ahead mentality. Ambitions are fine if born from a Kingdom-minded heart, but ambitions for selfish gain are dangerous. They are not the heart God is looking for.

Again, I am not saying aspiration is a bad thing. First Timothy 3:1 even encourages aspiration. But you must evaluate your *why*. Do you want to lead in order to be admired for your influence, or do you want to lead because you want to point people to Christ? If the latter, great! Run for it. If the former, it is time to recalibrate your heart. Timothy beautifully modeled this balance. He showed what it looks like to passionately pursue the call of God and also surrender faithfully in any role. We would all do well to adopt such a spirit—a spirit that wants to be only where God wants us to be.

Whatever the current state of your heart, this will require some training, as Paul put it. Listen to what he told Timothy about striving for godliness instead of worldly pursuits:

> Have nothing to do with irreverent, silly myths. Rather train yourself for godliness; for while bodily training is of some value, godliness is of value in every way, as it holds promise for the present life and also for the life to come. The saying is trustworthy and deserving of full acceptance. For to this end we toil and strive, because we have our hope set on the living God, who is the Savior of all people, especially of those who believe.
>
> 1 Timothy 4:7–10

Train for godliness; make it your daily practice. Stop toiling away for what will only leave you empty. As Solomon said, it is "chasing after the wind" (Ecclesiastes 1:14 NIV). Essentially, it is fruitless and unattainable, because it will never be enough. Only godliness has eternal value in the Kingdom.

Aquila and Priscilla

Aquila and Priscilla would be considered couple goals for sure! We do not know much about their past other than they were Jews living in Rome, but after Claudius commanded all Jews to leave the city, they moved to Corinth. It was there they met Paul. Whether or not they were Christians before they met Paul, we do not know, either. In Acts 18, where we first encounter them, they are serving in the same occupation as Paul—tentmakers—and so Paul stayed with them for a while. It was the start of a beautiful friendship.

When Paul left Corinth, Aquila and Priscilla went with him to Ephesus. While Paul continued on, they stayed in Ephesus to help lead the church there. Some think they may have eventually returned to Rome, but it is likely they remained in Ephesus permanently.

Missions work and evangelism may receive a lot of prestige in the church, but those callings are no more effective or righteous than staying in one place and sending down deep roots. Aquila and Priscilla's ministry flourished because they served faithfully where God planted them and were devoted to building their local church. We read in Acts 18 that Aquila and Priscilla were instrumental in helping the evangelist Apollos develop a strong theological foundation, and Paul mentions in Romans 16:4 that they risked their lives for him. God used them mightily because they were obedient to serve with longevity.

While generations before us plugged themselves into their jobs and churches for a lifetime, the tendency in this modern era is to be always bouncing around, looking for the next best thing. But that is not always God's plan. For many of us, faithful service to the Kingdom means getting plugged into our local church and serving wherever the need might be, like Aquila and Priscilla or like Roger and Joy. If that is what God is calling you to do in this season, or beyond, a "Here I am" spirit means getting planted and staying planted in spite of those you see coming and going around you.

Do not minimize the value found in embracing where God has sent you, whether for a season or an extended period. When you are walking in His will, He will extend your reach and multiply your impact beyond what you could accomplish on your own.

The Disciples

The disciples are some of the most influential and pivotal characters in the New Testament. They lived and breathed with Christ while on earth, and when He left, they led the early Church. In the end, ten were martyred for their faith. The echo of their bold "Here I am" declarations—made with their lives and dying breaths—can be heard even today.

Peter

While Peter was a pillar in the early Church, he was not always so steady. When Jesus was on earth, Peter often fumbled along the way. After the resurrection, however, his "Here I am" heart really shined.

If Peter's story speaks to one person, it is certainly the Christian who has fumbled a bit too. Peter denied Jesus three times the night He was captured. He kept his distance and chose not to engage while Christ went to the cross, but afterward he was keenly aware of how he had failed his Savior. When Jesus returned to earth after the resurrection, He went to the disciples and extended forgiveness and restoration to Peter. Let's take a look at what happened.

> Jesus said to Simon Peter, "Simon, son of John, do you love me more than these?" He said to him, "Yes, Lord; you know that I love you." He said to him, "Feed my lambs." He said to him a second time, "Simon, son of John, do you love me?" He said to him, "Yes, Lord; you know that I love you." He said to him, "Tend my sheep." He said to him the third time, "Simon, son of John, do you love me?" Peter was grieved because he said to him the third time, "Do you love me?" and he said to him, "Lord, you know everything; you know that I love you." Jesus said to him, "Feed my sheep." . . . And after saying this he said to him, 'Follow me.'"

John 21:15–17, 19

What a picture of redemption. Peter had denied Jesus three times before His death, and now Jesus was giving him three opportunities to commit to and affirm his love for Him and His people.

The disciple had made mistakes, yes; Jesus was speaking to that part of his story when he called Peter "Simon," the name he went by before he made his declaration of faith in "Christ, the Son of the living God" (Matthew 16:16). But Jesus reminded Peter of who he had been and who he was, and He demonstrated that the disciple would go forth as Peter, meaning "rock."

Indeed, Peter would go on to be a rock in the early Church. He would be steady and foundational, a mighty pillar in God's redemptive plan for mankind. Was Peter perfect after this experience? No—and neither will you be this side of heaven. But God changed who he was into who he was meant to be, who God saw him to be. The same can happen for you.

If you have wavered but want to make a firm commitment to be a rock for Jesus, take heart! Your past does not disqualify you from Kingdom purpose moving forward. God wants to use you and has incredible purpose for a devoted believer like yourself. You can commit to Him with loyalty now and walk faithfully in the plans He has for you. His mercies are new every day, and today is a new day!

James

James, one of the sons of Zebedee and brother of the disciple John, was one of the early followers of Christ. He was a fisherman with Peter, Andrew and John, and he met Jesus early on in His earthly ministry. He was also included in Jesus' inner circle—part of the small group in close relationship with Jesus who experienced miraculous moments, such as when Jesus was transfigured on the mountain. We honestly do not get a lot of commentary about him outside of his time with Jesus, but we do know that he was martyred early on. After Jesus ascended to heaven and as the disciples set out to establish the Church, Herod had James murdered by sword. He was the first of the disciples killed.

This alone says so much about James' heart. When Jesus asked them to go make disciples, James took it seriously. He had to have been proclaiming Jesus as the Savior—and doing so boldly—for the king to take notice of him. Even unto death, he was faithful to his Jesus. Perhaps Jesus saw the tremendous witness he would become, which is why he gave him the name "son of thunder." He was a powerful force for the Kingdom of God.

Life often calls out of us our real commitment to Christ. In the hardest and most dire moments, will you remain faithful and true to the cross? James' "Here I am" heart met death, but it was that kind of surrender that caused people to take notice of the Gospel. I pray that you and I can be like James in our level of surrender. May we be such a witness for the Gospel that the enemy takes notice.

John

John was "the disciple whom Jesus loved" (John 13:23 NIV). Also a son of Zebedee and part of Jesus' inner circle, John enjoyed a unique closeness with Christ while He was on earth. The Bible shows us that he leaned on Jesus at the Last Supper and was entrusted with the care of Jesus' mother at the cross. After the resurrection, John was the first disciple to reach the empty tomb, first to believe in the resurrection and first to recognize the risen Christ. After this point we do not see him much in the Scriptures, but we do know, through Paul, that he often worked with Peter and was instrumental in establishing the early Church (Galatians 2:9).

In addition to his ministry, John is often credited as the author of the gospel of John, the letters of John and the book of Revelation. It is widely believed that he was not martyred but lived a long life devoted to Christ.

John was intimately aware of just how precious Jesus was. He wanted to be as close to Jesus as possible, and indeed he was.

This kind of heart is why he was entrusted with Mary and why he was the first to believe after the resurrection. He intimately knew Christ. His "Here I am" was a personal one, not only to what Jesus asked of John in ministry but also in friendship.

It begs us to ask of ourselves, How close am I to Jesus? Whatever the answer, strive to be closer. Know him, as John did, and serve Him with all your heart.

Philip and Andrew

How often do you wait for a green light or for the circumstances to be perfect before talking to someone about Jesus? I have been there! Both Philip and Andrew are prime examples, however, of how naturally—and effectively—evangelism can happen when we are passionate about Christ.

Andrew was Peter's brother and the first to follow Jesus. Before that he was a disciple of John the Baptist, but when he heard John exclaim, "Behold, the Lamb of God," he committed to follow Jesus (John 1:36–37, 40). From the beginning, Andrew was passionate about bringing people to Christ. His first convert was his brother, Simon Peter, but he is also noted in Scripture for bringing others to Jesus, certainly showing his heart to lead people to the Savior.

Likewise, Jesus called Philip to come follow Him early in His ministry (John 1:43). Philip's commitment was immediate. As soon as Jesus called him, he followed and witnessed to Nathanael, who joined the fold. Philip did not wait for instructions about how to share his faith; he simply believed Jesus, and the overflow of his faithful heart was a light to others.

While there is often wisdom in discerning how best to witness to someone (i.e., through words or action), Andrew and Philip remind us not to overcomplicate the process. Evangelism must always be a natural outflow of your love and devotion to Christ. If you are waiting for the perfect circumstances to tell people about Jesus, you are going to miss so many opportunities to lead people to Christ and fulfill your mission to make disciples. Do not hesitate to be a witness. May your love and faith in Christ compel you to lead people to Him now!

Thomas

Have you heard the term "doubting Thomas"? Now you know where it comes from. Though he sometimes gets a bad rap because after the resurrection of Christ he would not believe until he saw Jesus himself, Thomas has some noteworthy moments of faith.

In John 11 we read about the death of Lazarus and how Jesus raised him from the dead. When Jesus heard that Lazarus was dead, all of the disciples tried to persuade him not to go visit his friend out of fear of the Jews—all but one. Thomas replied, "Let us also go, that we may die with him" (v. 16). In the face of fear, Thomas showed courage and devotion. He was loyal.

We do not know why he was not there to see Christ resurrected with the rest of the disciples, nor why he doubted, but it was perhaps because of such determined loyalty. I certainly do not want to be found guilty of adding to the Bible, but I do like to give people the benefit of the doubt. As someone who is fiercely loyal, I might pull away too after such a heartbreaking blow to process what happened. Perhaps Thomas was so fiercely loyal and the loss so hard that he pulled away and then asked for proof because he was protecting his heart. Regardless of why he seemed reluctant to believe, Thomas' response to meeting the resurrected Christ was his own version of a "Here I am." When Jesus lovingly told the disciple, "'Do not disbelieve, but believe,' Thomas answered him, 'My Lord and my God!'" (John 20:27–28).

Over and over again the world will offer us opportunities to doubt our Savior. It will tempt us to close ourselves off from faithful fellowship and protect ourselves from hurt or error. It will whisper that our past failures disqualify us from bearing any kind of fruit for the Kingdom of God. In some instances it will threaten our very well-being. Each of the men and women whose lives and faith we have examined in the chapter experienced the same temptations—and each of them chose to forge ahead in faith and obedience. They overcame obstacles, conquered doubt and stared down certain death to declare, "Here I am, Lord." Their lives and legacies are a call to action for us today. When you make your own declaration and then walk out the call of God on your life, you will find yourself stepping into the full, flourishing, eternal life God destined just for you.

Part Three

THE GREAT "HERE I AM"

11

THE SON OF GOD OBEYS

There is no better example of a "Here I am" than the one Christ offered each and every day of His life. No one has ever been more obedient than Jesus. He was fully God, yes, but He was also fully man while here on earth. And He set aside His own comfort for the will of the Father so that mankind might be rescued from their sin. Paul put it this way in his letter to the Philippians:

> He had equal status with God but didn't think so much of himself that he had to cling to the advantages of that status no matter what. Not at all. When the time came, he set aside the privileges of deity and took on the status of a slave, became human! Having become human, he stayed human. It was an incredibly humbling process. He didn't claim special privileges. Instead, he lived a selfless, obedient life and then died a selfless, obedient death—and the worst kind of death at that—a crucifixion. Because of that obedience, God lifted him high and honored him far beyond anyone or anything, ever, so that all created beings in heaven and on earth—even those long ago

dead and buried—will bow in worship before this Jesus Christ, and call out in praise that he is the Master of all, to the glorious honor of God the Father.

Philippians 2:5–11 MESSAGE

This passage about Jesus says it all. He set aside His privileges as the Son of God and became obedient to the Father, even unto death. His submission to God, patience and servanthood have a lot to teach us about how we should walk out our own faith and pursue the call and purposes of God in our lives.

How It All Began

For the first thirty years of His life, Jesus enjoyed a relatively normal and quiet existence in Nazareth with His family. John the Baptist was preparing the way for Christ by preaching His coming, and lots of people were getting baptized. Israel was experiencing a revival like no other in that day.

Then one day Jesus showed up at John the Baptist's camp meeting on the muddy banks of the Jordan River. Immediately, John knew who was standing before him—Jesus, the One he had preached about for so long and pointed others to. This Savior now stood before him, and everything was about to change. John exclaimed, "Behold, the Lamb of God, who takes away the sin of the world!" (John 1:29).

Then Jesus stepped forward to be baptized. We have already talked about Jesus' humble spirit in this moment and how He did not jump onto the scene and say, "I'm here!" No. Instead, He waited His turn and submitted to the water baptism John offered. Understandably, John was hesitant. "I need to be baptized by you, and do you come to me?" he asked Jesus (Matthew 3:14). But Christ sought John's baptism to "fulfill all righteousness," as He put it (v. 15). As He came out of the water, the heavens opened up, and a loud voice proclaimed, "This is my beloved Son, with whom I am well pleased" (v. 17).

After the baptism, Jesus went into the desert, and for forty days and nights He was tempted. He was put to the test. Satan took three shots to try to knock Jesus off His path, but he failed. Instead of submitting to each temptation, Jesus chose instead to submit Himself to God's plan for His life. Jesus stood firm in His trials, using the Word of God as a defensive tool and reaffirming with each declaration that He was available and obedient to God alone. Indeed, He was victorious!

His Earthly Ministry

Jesus spent three years ministering to the lost and broken. He saw people—and I mean, really saw them—and extended grace to all who would believe in Him. No one was exempt from His loving-kindness nor too far gone. His Gospel was for all—Jew and Gentile alike. Beth Moore beautifully encapsulates the kind of love Jesus has for us:

> Who else could name every single thing you've ever done and you'd want everyone to meet him? The only one with the right to rob us of all dignity robes us with it instead.[1]

It would take pages I do not have to illustrate the fullness of Jesus' "Here I am" attitude in those three years He spent in ministry. Instead, we will focus on the highlights—key moments of His obedience to the Father during His time on earth.

The Wedding at Cana

The wedding at Cana was the site of Jesus' first recorded miracle in the Scriptures. Though a quiet act likely unbeknownst to most attendees at the wedding, it nonetheless had significant impact for those who were witnesses to the miracle. More than that, it is a poignant example to us today of how Jesus was faithful, even in the small things.

There with Jesus were His mom, brothers and the five disciples He had called up till that point. He did not have much of a following yet, and His tribe was small. His family knew of His deity, and certainly the disciples believed He was who He said He was, but they had yet to see Him demonstrate His power. That was about to change.

When Mary requested that Jesus do something about the lack of wine, He responded in a way that expressed He only operated on the Father's timeline. To turn the water into wine—to perform such a miracle—meant it was acceptable to the Father, whom He obeyed in every way. If that meant a quiet act of turning water into wine as opposed to some vivid miracle witnessed by many, then Jesus did it.

There is more to the story, as Warren Wiersbe explains:

> This miracle also presents a practical lesson in service for God. The water turned into wine because the servants cooperated with Jesus and obeyed His commands. Several of the signs in John's Gospel involve the cooperation of man and God: the feeding of the 5,000 (John 6), the healing of the man born blind (John 9), and the raising of Lazarus (John 11). Whether we pass out bread, wash away mud, or roll away the stone, we are assisting Him in performing a miracle.[2]

Jesus was modeling the importance of operating in submission to the Father. Then and now, He is not asking humanity to do anything He did not also do Himself. He showed exactly what it looks like to live a life that puts God's will above our own.

The Woman at the Well

Jesus' conversation with the Samaritan woman at the well was nothing short of scandalous. When she came to the well where

He rested, Jesus said to her, "Give me a drink" (John 4:7). The woman was obviously surprised that He was speaking to her. In those days, Jews did not speak to Samaritans because they were considered unclean. But Jesus loved everyone, and He was not about to back down from a ministry opportunity. He put culture aside and spoke directly to the woman. What's more, He knew all of her past mistakes and still extended grace to her. As a result of His bold obedience, the woman's life was changed, and she immediately went to tell others about Him.

When it comes to God's love, nobody is off limits. He loves the underdogs, the misfits, the outcasts and those who seem unlovable. And you are called to them, too. He is calling you to love those who are unloved, to sacrifice for your neighbor, give to your enemy and to get involved in messy and uncomfortable conversations for the sake of the cross. He is asking you to go and care for those most unlike you, because love is magnified in no greater way than this.

When we are serving God fully, our priorities will be the same as Jesus': to obey the Father and extend grace to the hurting and lost. If Jesus was not held back by cultural norms or what others thought about Him in pursuit of these goals, neither should we be. This means your "Here I am" moment might look a bit different from the norm, but that is okay; Jesus' did too.

The next passage explains how Jesus overcame the pull of the world and the pressure to please others. When the disciples asked Jesus to eat, He replied, "I have food to eat that you do not know about" (John 4:32). The men were understandably confused, so Jesus clarified: "My food is to do the will of him who sent me and to accomplish his work" (v. 34). This no doubt shows just how obedient Jesus was to the Father, but it also tells us that Jesus made a daily decision to prioritize His spiritual walk over His fleshly needs. He was able to block out others' opinions and hone in on God's voice because He cultivated a lifestyle oriented toward hearing from Him.

This begs you and me to ask ourselves, Am I feeding my physical or spiritual desires? Am I submitting to God or to the world? When we learn to walk with God and nourish our spirits, we will find new levels of both fulfillment and fruitfulness for the Kingdom.

The Death of Lazarus

Lazarus was a close friend to Jesus, so it was an example of divine self-control that Jesus chose not to run to his friend's side when he found out Lazarus was gravely ill. His human nature likely compelled Him to go right away to save him from death. But following the will of the Father, He waited. Two days He waited to go. And when He got to Bethany, Lazarus was dead.

When Jesus saw the mourners in front of the tomb where Lazarus lay dead, it was a difficult experience for Him. It probably did not help that Mary pointed out, "Lord, if you had been here, my brother would not have died" (John 11:32). There, in front of the crowd gathered to mourn Lazarus, Jesus wept (v. 35). But God had a plan.

Instead of healing the sick—a miracle Jesus had performed many times previously—He raised Lazarus from the dead. The incredible nature of the miracle was as significant as the timing. Jesus brought Lazarus back from the dead just before He would go to the cross. Because He was obedient to the Father's will instead of doing what He wanted to do for a friend, Jesus was able to demonstrate the power of God not only to heal but to revive, and He simultaneously foreshadowed His own resurrection.

This account is the perfect example of when "Here I am" can be expressed through a willingness to wait patiently on God's plan. Sometimes stepping out in faith might mean holding back and waiting for the right time. When you find yourself growing impatient that things are not unfolding according to your plan, remember that what seems good to you may be better approached another away. Going forth requires patience and trust, as well as surrender to the Lord.

Washing the Disciples' Feet

Covered with the dust from the streets, the feet of the disciples were dirty and marked with cuts as they entered the room for the Last Supper. It was a servant's job to wash the feet of those entering the house, but no servant was to be found. As the disciples reclined next to each other while they ate at the dinner table, Jesus quietly got up, laid aside His outer garments, took up a towel and carried the basin of water over to Simon Peter. Jesus, the Son of God, humbled Himself to wash the grime and dirt off of the feet of each man one by one.

The task, however disagreeable, had to be done, and only Jesus took the initiative to see it accomplished. It was out of love He performed the duties of a slave. Among a group of men who often quarreled over greatness, Jesus set the example of service leadership and love instead of strife. It is also a beautiful picture of His "Here I am" spirit.

As if that was not a powerful enough object lesson, later the same evening Jesus continued His ministry to the gathered disciples. After He had just given an example of His love at dinner, He proclaimed, "A new commandment I give to you, that you love one another: just as I have loved you, you also are to love another. By this all people will know that you are my disciples, if you have love for one another" (John 13:34–35). This was how He wanted to leave the men He had grown close to over the last three years. *This is how I love.* It was an act to remember forever.

Jesus is calling all people to have this same kind of love. It is a love that initiates when others sit back, a love that humbles you to face what may seem unlovely and serve those in positions underneath you, a love that acts even with the knowledge of another's impure motives or betrayal and a love that cleanses. It is unconditional love.

This kind of love is not always easy, but it is always worth it because God is glorified. It is a witness to the ungodly. So set the example of service to those around you, whether friends or strangers. Show love by taking the initiative to humble yourself and cleanse people. Put others before yourself, and let God shine. In this self-serve world, your service will stand out.

His Death and Resurrection

Jesus' final act of obedience to God—His sacrifice—demonstrates His "Here I am" attitude more than any other. He understood the cross would be the hardest thing He ever did, yet He went willingly. Jesus did not have to do any of what He did, but He loved you so much that sacrifice was a small price if it meant the veil could be torn so you could experience intimate fellowship with the Father. If it meant you could be saved.

As He prayed in the Garden of Gethsemane on the night He was betrayed, Jesus knew what was coming. He knew He would be beaten, humiliated, taunted and hung on a cross to die. But that was not even the worst of it. The greatest burden was that He who knew no sin was about to experience sin for the first time—and not just one sin but all sin. There is no greater weight of burden than all the sins of mankind, and only Jesus could ever carry it. He is the perfect Lamb, the only one who could atone for our mess. His prayer on the Mount of Olives no doubt gives us insight into what He knew was to take place.

Father, if you are willing, remove this cup from me. Nevertheless, not my will, but yours, be done.

Luke 22:42

Luke describes that as He prayed these words, Jesus was on His knees and that His "sweat became like great drops of blood falling down to the ground" (Luke 22:44). He suffered such agony in these private moments that He literally bled. It is a condition called hematidrosis. Under intense emotional stress, small blood vessels rupture in the sweat glands and produce a mixture of blood and sweat. It is rare, but it can happen under severe burden, which was the case that night.

Jesus knew what He had to do, but it was still overwhelming. Even when Jesus prayed for the cup to pass from Him—for a way to avoid the pain that was ahead of Him—He still knew the only thing that mattered was His Father's will. If it meant dying on a cross with the weight of the world on Him, then He would do it. There in the garden and with every breath He took until His death, Jesus said, "Here I am, Lord," with His heart and life.

We can learn so much from Jesus' "Here I am" spirit. He was God, but clothed in humanity, He also served the Father in all humility and obedience. No task was too great or small for Him to carry out. No step of obedience was too much for God to ask of Him. No command from the Father was too much to bear. Jesus understood that the Father is good, and His plan is good. That was enough for Him. May it be enough for us, too.

No matter what lies ahead, if God has called you to it, then it is good. It is not promised to be easy or without pain, but it will be good. And He can take even the most hurtful, messy and dismal circumstances and use them for His purposes.

And we know that for those who love God all things work together for good, for those who are called according to his purpose.

Romans 8:28

God sees you, loves you and is working "all things . . . together" for your good. Do you trust Him? Will you trust Him? If you have any doubt, then the next chapter should surely change your mind and show you just how much He cares for you.

12

GOD'S GREAT "HERE I AM"

When I gave birth to my son, Roman, and held him in my arms for the first time, I never thought that only days later I would end up in the intensive care unit wondering if I would ever see him again.

Everything went fairly normal during labor and delivery. I gave birth on a warm Friday night and was sent home Sunday afternoon. Those first few days in the hospital with my precious baby boy were some of the most joyful of my life—even with the lack of sleep! But just before they discharged me, I started feeling sick to the point I could barely stand. I was assured it was the lack of sleep and having just had a baby, so they sent me home to get some rest. I clocked in a few hours of sleep once we got to our house and felt better by dinnertime with my parents. I thought I was on the up-and-up and was really looking forward to our first night at home as a family of three.

That night around nine o'clock as we settled into our room and placed Roman in the cradle next to our bed, I started feeling sick again. This time around it was far more intense. Within thirty minutes I went from a two to a nine on the pain scale.

It felt like I was having one nonstop contraction. I had never been to the emergency room in my life, but I knew something was not right and needed to go.

With great sorrow in my heart I kissed my newborn good-bye and left him in the care of my parents, and Ryan rushed me to the emergency room. Around three o'clock that morning I was admitted to the intensive care unit. I stayed there for the next three days with a rare blood clot—so rare they were not quite sure how to treat it.

It was a whirlwind of a week. From the emotional high of giving birth to the moments when I was not sure if I was going to make it, Ryan was close to me through it all. He held my hand as pain medications did not help and I cried out in agony. He slept on the couch in the hospital after I delivered and then again when I was back in ICU, and he prayed with me each day. When we got home, he lovingly took care of our baby while I recovered. I do not think we have ever been as close as we were during that season of our lives. He was there by my side in a very difficult time in my life and was a rock-solid support system for our family. I will never forget the way he loved and served our family in that season.

Referring to Eve in Genesis 2:18, God told Adam He would make him an *ezer kenegdo*. The Hebrew term is most often translated as "helper" or "companion," but some commentators have pointed out that those words do not begin to address the real meaning of the phrase. Robert Alter, a Hebrew scholar who has devoted much of his career to studying this and other passages in Genesis, suggests a better translation is "sustainer beside him."[1] Though God was describing Eve when He called her Adam's *ezer kenegdo*—his "lifesaver," as John Eldredge renders it[2]—the term paints a perfect picture of the role Ryan played in my life during that time. When I needed him, he was there beside me, lifting me up and bearing me onward.

Ryan's love and service to me when I needed them most were a direct reflection of the unconditional love and servant heart of God. In fact, the only other times *ezer* appears in the Bible are descriptions of the Father. Eldredge points out that "most of the contexts are life and death . . . and God is your only hope. Your *ezer*. If he is not there beside you . . . you are dead."[3]

Sometimes we wonder if God is there for us in our valleys and storms. We ask where He is because we feel alone. But the Bible makes it clear time and time again that God is standing at the door, ready to be there for us when we call upon Him. Whether or not we perceive His presence, He is there with us— yes, as a helper and companion, but also as our Savior. If you need any proof of this, look no further than God the Father's own "Here I am" moment in the book of Isaiah.

A Lost Nation

The people of Israel were in distress. They had disobeyed the Lord and failed to heed the warnings of the prophets, removing themselves from His protection. Now, lost and wandering, the temple at Jerusalem in ruins, God's favored people cried out for help and any sign of His favor, but He was silent.

In an attempt to regain His favor, the people chose to reinstitute religious rituals, like fasting and prayer. When it did not make a difference, they clamored, "Why do we fast and you don't look our way? Why do we humble ourselves and you don't even notice?" (Isaiah 58:3 MESSAGE). They could not understand why their good deeds did not result in God's blessings. Then God told them why.

> The bottom line on your "fast days" is profit. You drive your employees much too hard. You fast, but at the same time you bicker and fight. You fast, but you swing a mean fist. The kind of fasting you do won't get your prayers off the ground. Do

you think this is the kind of fast day I'm after: a day to show off humility? To put on a pious long face and parade around solemnly in black? Do you call that fasting, a fast day that I, GOD, would like?

Isaiah 58:3–5 MESSAGE

The people questioned God's faithfulness, and yet their lives represented only selfishness and self-righteousness. They wanted to treat others poorly, pursue self-interest and live for the glory of themselves instead of the glory of the Father—and then they wondered why God was not in it. In short, Israel touted their morality, but their hearts were far from God.

They failed to understand that no religious act done for selfish gain or promotion is considered pure and acceptable to God. Look at the Pharisees and how Jesus responded to them. The Father is not looking for empty commitments and lofty words; He wants real love. It is the heart He is after.

Going through the motions is rarely enough. Actions without heart often fall flat, at least eventually. Employees who check off all their tasks but have no passion for the work will never go above and beyond or give it their all. Perhaps your spouse does his or her fair share around the house, but if he fails to express his love for you, you are going to have a hard time, right? This is where Israel was, and God took notice.

The Father knew they could be more, be better, and called them to a more noble way of life.

This is the kind of fast day I'm after: to break the chains of injustice, get rid of exploitation in the workplace, free the oppressed, cancel debts. What I'm interested in seeing you do is: sharing your food with the hungry, inviting the homeless poor into your homes, putting clothes on the shivering ill-clad, being available to your own families. Do this and the lights will turn on, and your lives will turn around at once.

Your righteousness will pave your way. The GOD of glory will
secure your passage.

Isaiah 58:6–9 MESSAGE

Israel was wondering where God was in the middle of their dif-
ficulty, and it turned out the answer was simple: He was there
all along; they just could not see or hear Him moving because
the eyes and ears of their hearts were fixed on themselves instead of outward. Their lives were not devoted to Him, nor were
their prayers made with a pure heart that was committed to the
purposes of God. As a result, their acts of religion bore no fruit.

All along, God had been waiting to step into the lives of His
people once again and turn them around "at once." All He
needed was for them to change their motives and make a decision
to serve Him and others genuinely instead of serving themselves.
He was calling them to a life that canceled debts, served the poor
and treated others warmly. He was asking for their whole hearts.

If you want God to show up powerfully in your life, you must
first look inward. Who is on the throne of your heart? Is it you,
or is it the Lord? How you answer that question will determine
whether the outflow of your life is righteous or merely religious.
It will also determine how strongly you sense God's presence
with you when you most need Him.

A Willing God

All of this leads us to the great and powerful "Here I am" moment from God. After giving the Israelites an itemized list of
what real, godly love would look like in action, God not only
promised His people that He would protect them; He promised
them Himself: "Then when you pray, GOD will answer. You will
call out for help and I'll say, '*Here I am*'" (Isaiah 58:9 MESSAGE,
emphasis added).

That phrase, when uttered by God, can move mountains and make a way in the desert. When the Father expresses those three words, things happen. Our lives and circumstances change.

Commentator Matthew Henry offers this insight:

> When God calls to us by his word it becomes us to say, *Here we are; what saith our Lord unto his servants?* But that God should say to us, *Behold me, here I am,* is strange. When we cry to him, as if he were at a distance, he will let us know that he is near, even at our right hand, nearer than we thought he was. *It is I, be not afraid.* When danger is near our protector is nearer, *a very present help.* "Here I am, ready to give you what you want, and do for you what you desire; what have you to say to me?" God is attentive to the prayers of the upright, Ps. 130:2. No sooner do they call to him than he answers, *Ready, ready.* Wherever they are praying, God says, "Here I am hearing; I am *in the midst of you.*"[4]

If you are living a life devoted to Him and you call out His name, you can trust that God is there. You can have full confidence that the Father is ready to act on your behalf. He is your *ezer kenegdo*, the "lifesaver" who comes "alongside" you.[5]

Being a mother has taught me a lot about the heart of God and His "Here I am" love for us. The other day I was going through my closet to get rid of the clothes I do not wear anymore. (You know, the ones I have held on to for years believing I would wear again one day but have not!) As I did, Roman was running around the room and getting into every drawer he could get into. I scooped him up into my arms and dropped him on the bed in a body slam, which he loves. But then, in true toddler fashion, he quickly attempted to nose dive over the side, which was pretty high for him. Naturally, I caught him. Roman dove because he knew I would be there to keep him from harm.

In that moment I thought about how Roman never has to worry—nor should he. Roman trusts that his mom and dad will be there to catch him. He knows that Ryan and I will take care of the details of his life, like what he will eat and what it takes to keep him safe. He can flourish and even dive off the bed in his childlike wonder because I will be there.

The impact of that object lesson nearly brought me to my knees. I have been worrying quite a bit lately over some major life decisions Ryan and I have to make for our family. On top of that, I have been fighting to find healing for recent wounds inflicted by people I cared deeply for. I have felt as if I have been frantically dashing back and forth to keep all these balls in my life from dropping, which has left me frazzled, unsure and worried. As I looked into Roman's happy face there at my bedside, I realized that instead of maintaining my juggling act, I just want to rest in the Father and trust He is taking care of everything in my life. I want to rest in His perfect peace, in spite of what is going on around me.

This is what life is meant to be like for the believer. The Father does not want us to worry. Listen to what He tells us in Matthew 6:31–34 (NLT):

> So don't worry about these things, saying, "What will we eat? What will we drink? What will we wear?" These things dominate the thoughts of unbelievers, but your heavenly Father already knows all your needs. Seek the Kingdom of God above all else, and live righteously, and he will give you everything you need. So don't worry about tomorrow, for tomorrow will bring its own worries. Today's trouble is enough for today.

Just as I want Roman to know Ryan and I will take care of all his needs, the Father wants you and me to trust that He will handle all the details of our lives. He wants us to have that same childlike faith and wonder and to trust Him—really trust in His provision, and then rest in Him. All He asks is that we put Him first and obey His command to love our neighbor as ourselves. If we do this, He will be right there whenever we call.

This is what He promised the people of Israel. It would have been enough for Him to assure them that when they changed their hearts and called on Him their "lives would turn around at once" (Isaiah 58:8 MESSAGE). But He went on, repeating His promise and elaborating on the powerful result of choosing to serve Him wholeheartedly:

> *If* you get rid of unfair practices, quit blaming victims, quit gossiping about other people's sins, *if* you are generous with the hungry and start giving yourselves to the down-and-out, your lives will begin to glow in the darkness, your shadowed lives will be bathed in sunlight. I will always show you where to go. I'll give you a full life in the emptiest of places—firm muscles, strong bones. You will be like a well-watered garden, a gurgling spring that never runs dry. You will use the old rubble of past lives to build anew, rebuild the foundations from out of your past. You will be known as those who can fix anything, restore old ruins, rebuild and renovate, make the community livable again. *If* you watch your step on the Sabbath and don't use my holy day for personal advantage, *if* you treat the Sabbath as a day of joy, GOD's holy day as a celebration, *if* you honor it by refusing "business as usual," making money, running here and there—*then* you will be free to enjoy GOD! Oh, I'll make you ride high and soar above it all. I'll make you feast on the inheritance of your ancestor Jacob. Yes! GOD says so!
>
> Isaiah 58:9–14 MESSAGE, emphasis added

If you have not quite caught it yet, there is an *if* tied to His *then*. He says, *If you live for Me and live a life that is generous and pure, then I will be there.* It is not an unjust clause; it is simply a natural consequence. If your heart is a "Here I am" heart for Him, then naturally, His heart is to say "Here I am" to you.

Compare your heart with what God described to the Israelites. Are your motives pure? Is your heart centered on Him? Is pleasing Him and pointing others to the cross your main goal? If not, rest assured, God loves you anyway. He loves you so much that He died just to be there, right there, when you called on His name. But also know that His love is calling you to something greater. He has more blessings, more abundance and more freedom waiting for you if only you will turn away from the world, tune out the whispers of the enemy and your own insecurities and declare that you are His.

If you already have a heart that desires after the things of God, then that means you can cry out to your Father and know He will be there. He will walk through the valley with you, hold your hand in moments of pain and uncertainty, guide your steps and stand beside you in the darkest seasons of your life. No matter who you are, where you come from or what you are going through, nothing is impossible for you, because nothing is impossible for your Father. You can trust that He is taking care of all the details concerning your life and that, "Here I am," will be God's response to your call.

Will "Here I am" be your immediate response to His? God has great plans for you. You were created to be a torchbearer of God's goodness and faithfulness to mankind. You were created to be a powerful vessel for the Gospel. And He is not done with you yet. Now is your time to embrace your destiny as a "Here I am" kind of believer who will go anywhere for the cause of Christ. Be open to whatever God has in store for you and then step, with Him at your side, into the richness of His glorious plan to use you powerfully in His Kingdom.

NOTES

Chapter 1: The Noises in Our Heads

1. Rick Warren, *The Purpose Driven Life: What on Earth Am I Here For?* (Grand Rapids: Zondervan, 2002), 186.

2. John Eldridge, *Beautiful Outlaw: Experiencing the Playful, Disruptive, Extravagant Personality of Jesus* (New York: FaithWords, 2011), 111.

3. Arnold Cole and Pamela Caudill Ovwigho, Center for Bible Engagement, *Understanding the Bible Engagement Challenge: Scientific Evidence for the Power of 4*, December 2009, https://www.backtothebible.org/files /web/docs/cbe/Scientific_Evidence_for_the_Power_of_4.pdf.

4. E. M. Bounds, *Purpose in Prayer* (New Kensington, Penn.: Whitaker, 1997), 65.

Chapter 2: Fear and Doubts and Insecurity, Oh My!

1. Jonathan Martin, *How to Survive a Shipwreck: Help Is on the Way and Love Is Already Here* (Grand Rapids: Zondervan, 2016), 152–53.

2. Martin, *How to Survive a Shipwreck*, 155.

3. John MacArthur quoted in "33 Quotes about Doubt," *Christian Quotes*, https://www.christianquotes.info/quotes-by-topic/quotes-about-doubt /#axzz5P3Xbz7VU.

4. Jon Bloom, "Your Emotions Are a Gauge, Not a Guide," *Desiring God*, August 3, 2012, https://www.desiringgod.org/articles/your-emotions -are-a-gauge-not-a-guide.

Chapter 3: Abraham, the Patriarch

1. Eugene E. Carpenter and Philip W. Comfort, *Holman Treasury of Key Bible Words: 200 Greek and 200 Hebrew Words Defined and Explained* (Nashville: Broadman & Holman, 2000), 41.

2. Charles H. Spurgeon, *Faith in All Its Splendor* (Lafayette, Ind.: Sovereign Grace, 2006), 78.

Chapter 7: Isaiah, the Prophet

1. John MacArthur, "God's Man for a Nation in Crisis," *Grace to You*, November 19, 2000, https://www.gty.org/library/sermons-library/80-229.

Chapter 9: Old Testament Pillars

1. Beth Moore, *Daniel: Lives of Integrity, Words of Prophecy* (Nashville: LifeWay, 2006), DVD.

Chapter 11: The Son of God Obeys

1. Beth Moore (@BethMoorelpm), Instagram photo, September 10, 2018, https://www.instagram.com/p/Bni323CBkZW/.
2. W. W. Wiersbe, *The Bible Exposition Commentary* (Wheaton: Victor, 1996), Logos Bible Software.

Chapter 12: God's Great "Here I Am"

1. Robert Alter, quoted in John Eldredge, "God Is Our Ezer," *Ransomed Heart*, December 19, 2017, https://www.ransomedheart.com/daily-reading/god-our-ezer.
2. Eldredge, "God Is Our Ezer," *Ransomed Heart*, December 19, 2017, https://www.ransomedheart.com/daily-reading/god-our-ezer.
3. John Eldredge, "God Is Our Ezer."
4. Matthew Henry, *Matthew Henry's Commentary on the Whole Bible: Complete and Unabridged in One Volume* (Peabody, Mass.: Hendrickson, 1994). Logos Bible Software.
5. Eldredge, "God Is Our Ezer."

Brittany Rust has a passion to give encouragement to the world-weary believer through her writing, speaking and podcasting. She is the author of *Untouchable: Unraveling the Myth That You're Too Faithful to Fall*, founder of For the Mama Heart and host of the *Epic Fails* podcast. Brittany lives with her husband, Ryan, and son, Roman, in Castle Rock, Colorado.

Fun facts about Britt: She loves a good outdoor adventure, Andy's Frozen Custard, nibbling on her son's yummy cheeks and binge-watching *Downton Abbey*. She is also a big fan of road trips, great food and new experiences. Coffee is a must-have in life, and she prefers the mountains, rain and cooler weather. Learn more at www.brittanyrust.com.

Connect with Brittany Rust

Instagram: @brittanyrust
Facebook: /brittanyrustofficial
Twitter: @brittany_rust

If you are interested in booking Brittany to speak at your next event, visit www.brittanyrust.com.

Also from Brittany Rust

Too many Christians believe that they are too faithful to lie, steal, cheat or be lured into sexual temptation. Failing to fortify themselves, they end up doing those very things. Brittany Rust was one such person, and here she unravels the myth of being untouchable, gives practical ways to guard against temptation and shows that no one is beyond God's redeeming love.

Untouchable